DARKLING I LISTEN

The Last Days and Death of John Keats

DARKLING I LISTEN

The Last Days and Death of John Keats

JOHN EVANGELIST WALSH

ST. MARTIN'S PRESS ❄ NEW YORK

ISBN 0-312-22255-6

Library of Congress Cataloging-in-Publication Data

Walsh, John Evangelist, 1927–
    Darkling I Listen : the last days and death of John Keats / by
John Evangelist Walsh.
        p. cm.
    Includes bibliographical references (p.   ) and index.
    ISBN 0-312-22255-6
    1. Keats, John, 1795–1821—Journeys—Italy—Rome. 2. Keats, John,
1796–1821—Relations with women.   3. Keats, John, 1795–1821—Death
and burial.   4. British—Italy—Rome—History—19th century.
5. Poets, English—19th century—Biography.   6. Brawne, Fanny,
1800–1865.   7. Rome (Italy)—Biography.   I. Title.
PR4836.W275   1999
821'.7—dc21   99-14213
    [B]   CIP

Book design by James Sinclair

First edition: October 1999

Printed in the United States of America

DEDICATED

to the memory
of my brother

THOMAS MOORE WALSH
(1925–1992)

A poet himself, for him the name
of Keats was magic

Fair youth, beneath the trees, thou canst not leave
Thy song, nor ever can those trees be bare . . .

CONTENTS

Had he come here alone, he would have plunged into the grave in secret—we should never have known one syllable about him. This reflection alone repays me for all I have done.

—Joseph Severn

John Keats at age 22 (1817) in a pencil sketch made by his friend, the artist B. R. Haydon. (The background is here darkened.) The overhanging upper lip is more noticeable than in other depictions.

PROLOGUE: SECOND FLOOR, FRONT

Not the little that may have changed during the slow decades, but all that has stayed pretty much as it was, that is the pleasant sight that greets you on entering Rome's busy Piazza di Spagna. Come in walking or riding along one of the eight crowded feeder streets, or make your entrance as I did strolling down the broad, balustraded Spanish Steps. Either way, the long passage of years since John Keats drew his last agonized breath here is hardly noticeable.

Today over the cobblestones, in place of the horses' hooves and carriage wheels that back then set up such a clatter, there quietly glide rubber tires. But many old houses and buildings that were standing in Keats' time are still to be seen, in bustling use now as then. The crowds of shoppers hurrying from store to store are also there, and the loungers up and down the wide cascade of the elegant Steps, different only in dress. In the roadway at the plaza's center still stands the ornate fountain—a large open boat sculpted by Bernini—that the ailing Keats looking out his bedroom window could see and hear gently bubbling and burbling just below.

The house in which he died, No. 26, is also still very much in evidence, with his room, a small one on the second floor, now set apart as a memorial. The rest of the narrow, three-story building (three in addition to the ground floor) is no longer what it was then, separate apartments meant for private dwelling. Today the entire 250-year-old edifice is owned by the Keats–Shelley Memorial Association and is maintained as a museum, library, and cultural center.*

The precisely one hundred days that Keats resided at No. 26, cared for by a dedicated friend, forms a supremely affecting story of youthful hopes destroyed, an unhappy chronicle that is now among the best-known in all literary biography. Especially for those who value poetry as a natural force in life, the sad ending of such marvelous promise as Keats showed, just when that promise had begun to disclose itself more fully in finished work, remains infinitely touching. All the more surprising, then, is the fact that the story of Keats' last days and death has yet to be told at its fullest.

Of course the topic occupies a good deal of space in all the many excellent Keats biographies. But in those more elaborate contexts the attention sensibly centers on the productive years, his death being treated as one happening among many, even if the mournful concluding one. No separate book or monograph has ever been devoted to the events of those last days, a fact that, given Keats' continued popularity, must be listed among literature's more puzzling and regrettable oversights. A complete book on the subject obviously allows for the exercise of all that is now lacking: amplitude of approach, concentration on the telling detail, space in which to linger, to probe, to evoke.

Nor has the inherent human drama of the tragic tale, always felt of course in some degree by readers of the standard biographies, been portrayed in the manner it deserves. This is not in any way because of neglect or ineptness on the part of previous writers. It was only their much more restricted scope as to parts of the story that brought them up short, and the need to mingle literary criticism with the life. Still, the oversight is *there*, quite palpable to view on even cursory

---

*The tie with Shelley, of course, recognizes the mournful fact that both young poets died in Italy within eighteen months of each other (Shelley in 1822 in a boating accident), and both lie buried in the same Roman cemetery.

study, having some effect, it may be said, on three different areas. When the deficiency in these areas is repaired, a quite different color steals over the story—different in emphasis, in motivation, in the order of events and, so to express it, in the lighting of critical scenes.

Foremost of these neglected areas is the ever-fascinating matter of Keats and Fanny Brawne. This famous affair, so much and so often argued over because of Keats' strange epistolary writhings (in those riveting love letters, unpublished until a dozen years after Fanny's death), actually played a more decisive role in his final days than has yet been pictured. That deficiency, moreover, results from the altogether surprising fact that the affair itself is still in need of unraveling.

In Keats biography the century-long debate over Fanny's character and personality—controlled largely by the availability of the evidence—has been cast in extremes. First, with the publication of the love letters (his only, hers have not survived), one view came to the fore: she was shallow, heartless, vain, no fit companion for the poet. Much later, with publication of some of Fanny's letters to Keats' sister, came another view at the opposite pole: she was loving, generous, wise, the perfect mate for literary greatness. This view generally is the one prevailing now, sometimes with variations that allow the young lady to have had a minor fault or two.

In the following pages the curious tangle that was the love between the anguished poet and the intriguing Fanny is accorded its most searching investigation to date. The outcome, I trust, providing for the first time a framework of chronology and sequence, cause and effect, shows how humanly flawed was the relationship on both sides during the two and a half years it lasted. The degree and manner of Fanny's culpability is another thing, and I am aware that my own conclusions may grieve many, though on the evidence they are really unavoidable. A very young woman, she was neither so simple nor so complicated as she has been made to appear.

On a different level, my examination of Fanny is continued in Chapter 8, "The Girl He Left Behind." Here I trace her later life in relation to Keats matters, hoping by studying the woman she became to throw added light on her relations with the poet. This much, at least, I believe I can claim: everything that may presently be known of Fanny in her maturity is in Chapter 8 made plain, more so than in any previous source. I will add that in contrast to certain of Fanny's more sentimental adherents, I have not consciously pulled or stretched or tugged at the evidence to make it fit any particular pattern or portrait.

It is here, especially, that my essentially narrative approach to the story of Keats' last days finds its full warrant (of course a strictly factual narrative, but leaving much of the discussion to the Notes, along with source citations). The range of subtle complication to be met in the Fanny Brawne affair I feel can in no other way be so adequately unfolded. *Showing* how and why things happened, in the order they happened, where the needed information is at hand and is sufficiently rich in inference, is always more enlightening than *saying* that they happened, no matter how well analyzed. Conceivably with this approach a passage here and there may strike some readers as going too far (Fanny at her mirror in Chapter 2, say, or Keats' hemorrhage on the Hampstead stage in Chapter 3). But every detail in such reconstructed scenes rests on authentic fact, as my Notes in each case fully explain. Even where it would be easy to employ such touches unobtrusively, with smaller details, *no* fictional element intrudes on the narrative. The morning sun glinting off the houses in Naples harbor, for example, is not the musing of an author's idle fancy. It comes directly from an eyewitness, the friend who accompanied Keats on the voyage from England and who saw those white walls from the railing of the ship the day it arrived.

The second area needing review touches the question of Keats and religion, an old topic but one little discussed comparatively, and which now more than ever stands in need of an airing. An apostate Christian since his late teens and outspokenly anti-religious, when on his death-bed, wracked by suffering of the mind as much as of the body, he can be heard begging for the solace of spiritual belief, pitifully crying out for it. That fact, it would seem, has some real significance, meriting more than perfunctory attention. But this particular concluding scene, for some unguessed reason, is always by biographers passed over in relative silence.

The third area in need of an overhaul, more down to earth than the others and humanly much more compelling, not to say harrowing, concerns the nature and progress of Keats' disease, particularly how his physicians viewed it at the time. This is a subject today not easily grasped—all too often slighted, for instance, is one principal fact, that he did *not* go to Italy as a confirmed consumptive resigned to his fate and waiting to die. The truth is he went to Rome with good hopes of making a complete recovery from *whatever* was ailing him. On that matter even his doctors weren't sure, three of them judging that his symptoms were not dire, the bleeding included, and could indicate many things besides consumption. His was most probably a case, they all agreed, of "nervous irritability and general weakness," aggravated if not induced by overwork. Rest in a warm climate and "quietness of Mind" were about all he needed to set things right. Undeniable, of course, was Keats' tendency to lose himself in sustained bouts of study and feverish writing, jumping from one poem to another as the spirit took him.

Indeed, for a while in the comforting warmth and fascination of the Eternal City all Keats' hopes of making a full return to health and vigor seemed on the verge of coming true. Only when that pivotal fact is grasped do the events of his last hundred days, as they appeared to Keats himself as well as to the many friends he left waiting anxiously in London, come into proper focus.

The materials needed to rectify these shortcomings and extend the story's scope are not lacking: frank contemporary letters and other documents left by the parties most concerned, in addition to a number of later reminiscences. Though known to and used by critics and biographers for some time now, still buried in these sources is quite a large amount of basic information, all of it eminently recoverable. As with any document that is detailed and of fair length, close analysis can tease out a surprising amount of new fact even when working with sources well thumbed (and often it is only necessary to strike two new facts together to spark an unsuspected third). If in the first place those documents came hot from some sorely tried heart under pressure of the moment, they can be especially valuable—for instance, and primarily, the many anguished letters written home to England from No. 26 by the friend who watched over the dying man.

Of great collateral interest is the personal story of that friend, in its own way hardly less gripping. Throughout the lengthy ordeal in Rome he stayed with the doomed poet—the pronouncement of that doom itself coming to him as a shock—bravely easing those last terrible weeks and final pathetic moments. Ill-prepared by upbringing for his demanding role, this young man's faithful service to the dying poet and his long and happy life afterward do much to soften the harshness of the central tragedy. That story too is herein made explicit.

The setting in which the tragedy played itself out, two and a half rooms on the second floor of No. 26, was small indeed. But it was tasteful, well furnished, and convenient for getting around the sprawling city. The larger of the two rooms, some fifteen feet square, was barely adequate for its purpose. Looking out over one busy end of the elongated piazza, the western end, it served as a combined parlor-dining room with enough space to accommodate a couch-bed. There was no kitchen. Meals were brought in or prepared by the occupants themselves, though more often hot food was delivered from one of the local *trattorias*, especially the evening meal.

Keats' little bedroom, the death chamber, occupies an outside corner of the building and is fitted with two large casement windows. One window overlooks the main piazza, the other gives a sweeping view up and down the Spanish Steps, and the imposing church rising on their summit (its bells, for Keats, would have pleasantly punctuated some moment of every day). It is a narrow room, only about nine by twelve feet. An exceptionally high ceiling helps to diminish any permanent too-cramped feeling, though as the weary Keats soon found a sense of suffocation can't always be escaped. Painted on the ceiling in six rows, each row of six panels, are stylized roses, the identical sight glimpsed day after day and hour after hour by the glowing eyes of the bedridden poet as he thought of Fanny and waited impatiently to die. The floor is of red tile, too cold for the bare feet of a sick man, so at the time was probably covered by a scatter of rugs.

During his entire final month, now well aware of his fate, Keats never left this little room. He rose from his bed only now and then for an hour or so to sit listlessly staring out one of the windows. On my own visit there I spent time at both windows in turn, quietly observing the life below. As did Keats, I gazed down on the men and women hurrying past the house or trudging the Steps, some halting at the crowded flower-stall directly below me, others disappearing into shop doorways, a few lounging at the curious Bernini fountain, a great many streaming in every direction through the piazza. Drifting up to me came the steady if erratic rumbling noises of active life, blended into a single deep hum.

It had all happened so long ago. That was the melancholy thought that struck me when I first entered the old building and walked solemnly up the twisting stone staircase to the second floor. So long ago and in a vastly different world from mine. Long before Browning and Tennyson. Before Victoria. Before anyone really cared about Wordsworth or purchased his books. Before trains or the telegraph. Before such things as anaesthesia (how did they ever get through an operation without anaesthesia!). Before electricity, even before gaslight. Lit by candles or oil lamps, Keats' world was often a shadowy one.

In the little bedroom I had spent some minutes leaning on the sill of a window and peering vacantly down on the Steps, when a different mood began to take hold of me. It was a subtle sense of detachment, downright peculiar, as if at that moment I existed separate and alone. Something beyond mere height and distance had cut me off from the colorful and varied world below.

Turning, I sat looking for a while around the room. I noted the height of the walls and how their expanse was squeezed and reduced by the wide windows. My eyes drifted across the narrow width of the floor, measuring. Now where, I wondered, would his bed have been placed? Not much of a choice in a room like this. In that far corner, no doubt, well away from either window. As I stared at the empty corner, almost seeing the bed with its fevered occupant, my altered mood gradually and gently pressed out of mind all sense of the obtruding, intervening decades (seventeen of them and a little more).

It wasn't so long ago after all, I thought, the melancholy scene that played itself out in that very corner. Only yesterday.

DARKLING I LISTEN

The Last Days and Death of John Keats

Darkling I listen; and for many a time
   I have been half in love with easeful death,
Call'd him soft names in many a muséd rhyme,.
   To take into the air my quiet breath;
Now more than ever seems it rich to die,
   To cease upon the midnight . . .

From *Ode to a Nightingale*
by John Keats

ONE

DESTINATION ROME

A forest of bare masts, sails furled and cordage hanging slack, arose from the calm waters embraced within the wide-sweeping curve of busy Naples harbor.

By the hundreds, sailing craft lay crowded motionless together, bulky square riggers, tall schooners, and shallow sloops, down to slim *fellucas* with their angled sails. Awaiting berths ashore or the arrival of a port official, or off-loading freight or passengers into the tenders and skiffs that hurried up alongside, many ships were anchored literally within yards of each other. At intervals here and there a departing or arriving vessel moved slowly, its reduced canvas flapping noisily as it caught a stray wind.

Low on the horizon glowed the morning sun burning its way through the shimmering mist that hung on the mounting green terraces strung along the shoreline, not quite veiling the high, graceful cone of Vesuvius. Through the haze flashed the whitewashed walls of scattered buildings as they picked up sudden stabs of sunlight.

Off a point of land jutting into the harbor on the left, near imposing Castel d'Uovo, appeared a small, two-masted brig, a British flag flying at its mainmast peak. Moving carefully it slipped past vessel after vessel, slowing as it entered a vacant area, then with a great splash let go an anchor. Spindly masts and drooping yardarms naked, it came to a drifting halt, the broad stern circling lazily round the taut anchor cable, one more weathered wooden hull lost in the maze. Along its bow a string of letters spelled out the name *Maria Crowther*. In his cabin, Captain Thomas Walsh took down the ship's log and noted his safe arrival, adding the date: 21st October in the year of Our Lord 1820.

The brig had stood at rest only a few minutes when a launch was rowed up alongside carrying a port official. Alerted hours before by telescope to the *Crowther*'s approach, the authorities on shore were intent on reaching the new arrival before debarkation could begin. Making no effort to go aboard but standing in his launch and shouting up to Captain Walsh at the rail, the official delivered what proved to be a thoroughly unwelcome message. Some days before reports of a typhus epidemic in London had reached them. If the *Crowther* had set sail from that port less than two months ago, then she was declared to be in medical quarantine.

Captain Walsh replied that he'd been at sea only three weeks since leaving England, but had departed London more than six weeks before. He hoped that that amount of time would be considered sufficient. No, said the official, in that case an additional ten days in isolation were required. Until the afternoon of October 31st, no goods or passengers could be allowed off. Food and other necessary items could be sent aboard from shore. Mail would be delivered every other day if there was any. Outgoing letters would be permitted to leave the ship but were subject to fumigation, a process that did no damage, only yellowed the paper. He was sorry for the inconvenience. Those were Port's strict regulations.

The *Crowther* carried freight, not primarily passengers. It had accommodations for no more than five paying guests, and on this trip only four of the berths had been filled, two by women and two by men. Traveling separately, the women were a Mrs. Pidgeon, middle-aged and motherly, and a Miss Cotterell, a pretty eighteen-year-old on her way to join her brother, an English banker in Naples. The two men, both young, were friends traveling together. One was a

London artist of great promise named Joseph Severn, who at the young age of twenty-six had, only the year before, been awarded a gold medal by the Royal Academy (the prize picture, a large original oil, depicted the "Cave of Despair," a scene from Spenser's *Faerie Queen*). The other man was a published poet named John Keats, who at an even younger age, twenty-four, had three slim volumes to his credit (he would turn twenty-five the very day quarantine ended). At first destined for the medical profession, after several years' formal training Keats had left school. He was now fully committed to the life of writing, mainly poetry but eventually, he hoped, plays as well. He'd already finished one play—Drury Lane had been prompt to show interest—and had made a good start on another.

Dedicated and ambitious, both young men enjoyed much esteem within a restricted circle of London artists and writers, though neither man's name was at all familiar to the public at large. Of the two, Keats was the better known, his books having attracted some limited review attention (part of it harsh indeed) in a range of leading periodicals.

The dismal prospect of another ten days' confinement on board the small ship was not received gratefully by any of the four but for two in particular, Keats and Miss Cotterell, the news brought severe disappointment. Both were ailing and in some degree invalids. Neither had found the voyage from home to be an uninterrupted pleasure.

Miss Cotterell was a consumptive. Still in the early stages of the disease, like so many unfortunates before her, she had been ordered by her physician to seek the healing warmth of the Italian sun rather than chance another of England's wet, icy winters. Keats, also, had been sent to Italy by his doctor—living arrangements had been made for him at Rome, extending through the following spring—but his case was more problematic. Consumption might be involved, and it might not. A stomach impairment of some kind was thought to be equally possible or even a weakened heart. Aside from the worrying fact that a younger brother had died of consumption two years before (perhaps his mother as well, who had died a decade before that), there was no way to choose with certainty among the various symptoms.

During the past year, Keats had coughed up blood several times, indicating the rupture of a vessel in either stomach or lungs. But as every doctor was all too unhappily aware, in dealing with diseases of the lungs, or almost any of the internal organs, the medical practice of the day was very nearly helpless. Diagnosis was never more than tentative, a blind groping among a bewildering overlay of external signs, faint and equivocal. Treatment was no surer, resting on little more than each physician's instinct, more or less improvised. Medicines also were few, mostly ineffective narcotics in dilution along with an array of innocuous salts and syrups, none of them specific. But on one thing all were agreed, the insidious harm that could be inflicted on a weakened or unstable constitution by damp houses, cold winds, chilling rain, and bone-penetrating fog.

Miss Cotterell looked and frequently acted like the accepted picture of a consumptive: painfully frail, cheeks often flushed, moods alternating from gaiety to gloom, bursts of energy sinking into lassitude, occasional harsh coughing, wasting of flesh despite a regular diet. Keats on the other hand most of the time showed few outward signs of any disease. A man of short stature with a physique trimly compact and muscular, his movements were vigorous when required and displayed the easy grace of an athlete, which he'd been at school (well under the average male height of the day, he stood no more than an inch or two over five feet). His face, almost classically handsome though somewhat marred by a slightly prominent upper lip, reflected a vivid if controlled temperament. The large hazel eyes beamed a subtle combination of intelligence and strength and were devoid of the hectic glow that betrays the presence of a wasting fever. The portrait of health and well-being—curiously deceptive—was completed by thickly curling hair of a dark reddish brown that fell just below the ears.

Signs of Keats' ill health, beginning six months before, though apparently signaled well before that by a nagging sore throat, had never been more than intermittent, and usually of brief duration. On the interminable voyage to Italy he had experienced several bad turns, bringing up blood at each attack. Ample reason for these bad spells, however, was found in the cramped discomfort and annoyance of the ship's accommodations, suffered through six miserable weeks. Leaving London on September 18th, the ship had been much delayed in quitting English waters, held back by calms and contrary winds.

A single cabin, not large, housed all the passengers and the captain as well, the women's bunks being partioned off by a wide screen. Frequently during the voyage, because of the rough, squally weather the four had been forced to remain indoors, with the air in the shuttered cabin soon turning stale. This created a trying situation in which poor Miss Cotterell needed to have everything just the opposite of Keats. When the cabin windows were closed for any length of time, lamented Severn later, "she would faint and remain entirely insensible" for hours. Yet if the windows were thrown open, very rapidly Keats "would be taken with a cough . . . spitting up blood." Such worrisome attacks were brief enough in duration, but they tended to bring on some fever and troublesome night sweating.

To make matters a bit worse, in these emergencies the older Mrs. Pidgeon in a mild panic simply refused to help, even when Miss Cotterell "lay stiffened like a corpse." Between them, Keats and Severn would manage to get the prostrate young woman into her bunk—fully clothed, since Mrs. Pidgeon resolutely kept her distance—and would then stay by her giving what aid and sympathy they could. On these occasions Keats' medical training came in handy allowing him to relieve the worst of the lady's distress rather quickly. "Full a dozen times I have recovered this Lady and put her to bed," wrote Severn of the three-week crossing. Still, he added with a proper sense of fairness and gratitude, all the annoyance and inconvenience caused by Miss Cotterell when afflicted had been more than made up by her womanly charm and pleasant personality when well. Then she proved a delight for all, witty and "full of spirits . . . but for her we should have had more heaviness" on the long trip.

In this praise of Miss Cotterell's sprightly presence Keats gladly joined, though he did so with some reservations of a sort only he could really appreciate. Conscious every minute of his own uncertain state of health, in a letter home he admitted his utter distaste at being confronted daily and hourly by the young woman's pathetic condition. In the end he'd shown himself seriously upset and annoyed by it, though he never complained, not even privately to Severn. "All her bad symptoms have preyed upon me—they would have done so had I been in good health," he wrote, adding brusquely, "I shall feel a load off me when the lady vanishes out of my sight." The tone was unlike him.

The ten days of quarantine, as it turned out, despite the weather frequently becoming foul with sunless days of drifting mist and chilling rains, were not entirely miserable. On the second day Miss Cotterell's concerned brother showed up and no sooner learned of the quarantine than he surprised everyone by declaring he would join his sister aboard. Then he arranged for supplies of food, delicacies of all sorts along with fancy fruits and fish, to be delivered daily, vastly improving for all what had been the customary bare ship's table. He also expressed to the two young men his deep gratitude for the care and attention they had shown his sister. He would be both guide and host for them, he announced, when they came ashore. The offer was welcome for neither had bothered to arrange accomodations in the city for the few days of their stopover on the way to Rome.

Halfway through the quarantine an even livelier incident occurred when a party of men from a British warship, newly arrived in the bay, came to visit. Alongside the brig floated a launch rowed by ten sailors, and before anyone could issue a warning the naval officer in charge in the launch, a Lieutenant Sullivan, had clambered aboard. Eager for news of home, not waiting for permission, several of his men had followed, and the happy mingling of visitors and passengers on the deck had been in progress only a few minutes when another launch hurried up, this one carrying an excited port official. From the safety of the launch he announced that the naval party on board the brig, having broken quarantine, would have to remain there. The cabin's last empty bunk had been taken by Miss Cotterell's brother, so the abashed lieutenant had to spend his nights sleeping along with his men in the hold.

Never spacious, the little brig was now considerably crowded both day and night. But the added company actually helped the long hours to pass more pleasantly, especially the nights on deck when in good weather there was music and singing provided by the sailors. (Some of the bawdier songs, indulged when the women had gone indoors, considerably annoyed the gentlemanly Keats because he was sure they could be heard in the cabin. But he kept silent.) Some few days proved merry indeed as curious Italian visiters drifted up in small boats and with Cotterell rapidly translating, "all kinds of chaff went on," the steady exchange of jokes and jibes bringing "continued roars of laughter." In these freewheeling sessions not only Captain Walsh, Lieutenant Sullivan, and Cotterell took part, but Keats also as the four vied in firing off a stream of "witty puns and remarks." Keats, notoriously addicted to puns, later recalled, not at all sheepishly, that while in quarantine he perpetrated more puns "in one week than in any year of my life."

Moments of distraction were also found in the colorful activity swirling round the wide bay. Severn, his painter's eye eagerly scanning the unfamiliar scene, was utterly captivated, as he wrote, by "the splendid city of Naples and her terraced gardens and vineyards," and was especially entranced by "majestic Vesuvius, emitting strange writhing columns of smoke, golden at their sunlit fringes," the arresting tableau set off by "the azure foreground covered with all manner of white-sailed craft." There was entertainment, too, in the little boats, piled high with fruit and vegetables, that passed by or came up to barter, their occupants "playing upon their guitars and singing songs," all done in such a smiling, carefree spirit.

Keats was equally caught by these surroundings, so new and strange. Yet nagging worry over his future, as he admitted, had robbed him of the power and even the desire to dwell on it. "There is enough in this port of Naples to fill a quire of paper," he wrote three days after arriving, but he was unable to feel himself part of it. The scene spread around him, he said, "looks like a dream—every man who can row his boat and walk and talk seems a different being from myself." What a graphic account he might give of these wonders, "If I could once more feel myself a citizen of this world . . . O what a misery it is to have an intellect in splints!" Some few sights did catch his attention, however, which kept him staring fascinated from the ship's rail and which he did mention in a letter. The random fishermen sitting solitary in rowboats dotted round the bay was one such. Rapidly and repeatedly they would drop a single line into the calm blue surface, in seconds giving a hard yank and bringing up "a little fish much like an anchovy."

In his own first letter home from the ship, Severn duly reported on his friend's condition during the voyage—changeable and at times worrisome—ending with the doleful comment that Keats was just then in "a doubtful state—I cannot guess what this climate will do." He meant that the mere frustrations of quarantine, much worse on an overcrowded, one-cabin ship lying motionless within sight of an inviting shore, might well prove more harmful than expected. But those fears were borne out only in part. For much of the time Keats appeared actually to be enjoying his restricted life, though always with a feeling of reserve, as Severn noted, a sense of unspoken concern not related to his health. It was a relief to see Keats taken out of himself by his sharing in the ship's lighter moments, said Severn later, for hovering in the background was a hint of something disturbingly dark, all too noticeable when he was standing off by himself and staring at the water:

> He was often so distraught, with moreover so sad a look in his eyes, sometimes a starved, haunting expression that [it] bewildered me. Yet at the time I never fully understood how terrible were his mental sufferings, for so excruciating was the grief that was eating away at his life that he could speak of it to no one. He was profoundly depressed the day we went ashore at Naples, though he had been so eager to leave the ship and explore the beautiful city; indeed, I was more alarmed on his behalf that night

than even during the wretched three-days' storm in the Bay of Biscay.

The day the party was at last permitted to leave the ship, Keats' twenty-fifth birthday (about which, it seems, no mention was made by anyone), he was not at all elated by his release. Rather he showed himself to be, as Severn had put it, "profoundly depressed," unwilling as ever to talk of what was troubling him. Even the tireless friend who had watched over him on the voyage, who had so impulsively interrupted his own budding career to act as companion—in the process defying an angry father—couldn't draw him out. Such rigid silence, even toward his only confidante, the sympathetic Severn, in itself was a stark demonstration of how deep-seated was Keats' unspoken agitation. He was well aware of just how much he owed his admiring friend

Up to three days before departure of the *Maria Crowther* the affable Severn hadn't once thought he might be leaving England for distant shores. In London not counted among the poet's intimates, he was looked on by most in their circle as being of a somewhat immature turn of mind, naive, even shallow, in any case decidedly below Keats intellectually. It was a portrait which Severn's good-natured countenance and cheerful manner seemed to bear out—one acquaintance said that she couldn't imagine anything making him unhappy since she "never saw him for ten minutes serious." He was a lightweight personality, all agreed, unable to provide fit companionship, certainly not moral suport, for the poet regarded by many as destined for greatness (a rival to Shakespeare, his admirers soberly predicted). Who then *would* accompany the sick man? He had no family of his own available, his father also being dead and a surviving brother gone off to America. An only sister was too young and lived under the strict care of a legal guardian.

Those closer friends, it seems, were unable to arrange a hiatus in their busy lives, amounting to probably six full months. Consequently, as the day of departure neared it seemed unavoidable that

Keats must make the depressing move alone. There would be no familiar presence to lighten his exile, no congenial hand to serve him in the difficult days and hours almost certain to occur, even should his convalescence go smoothly. It was in desperation that a last-minute appeal had been made to Severn as the sole hope remaining. Almost eagerly, and full in the face of the elder Severn's disapproval, he agreed, throwing himself into a fever of preparation.

An ugly scene ensued, occurring on the very day Severn left home to join the waiting ship. Ordinarily a considerate, even-tempered man, the anguished father in those final minutes erupted. Shouting so that his voice rang through the house, unnerving his anxious wife and upsetting the other five children, he declared that his son was making a terrible mistake! Bad enough was the setting back of his regular art studies, going so well since the awarding of the gold medal. But to deliberately risk his own health by continued close contact with an ailing companion, someone hardly more than acquaintance! (Not everyone then believed in the contagious nature of disease, not even as to consumption, including most English doctors. Severn's father, apparently, was one who did.) In exasperation the father blocked the doorway, shoving his son back into the room and knocking him to the floor. Only the mother's pleas and the prompt intervention of another son averted further harm. In sore distress of spirit young Severn retrieved his bags and departed, grimly intent on keeping his word.

His sacrifice in going with Keats was real enough. But the interruption to his studies at home, as Severn readily admitted and as his friends understood, was not a complete disadvantage. His winning of the Academy's gold medal gave him the right to try for a coveted traveling fellowship, three years of freedom and independence fully funded, in which to pursue his art. He need only submit an original oil to the Academy and have it accepted by a panel of judges. For this demanding task a lengthy residence at Rome, then indisputably the world's art capital, would prove a great boon and he'd have until the spring of 1821 to complete the picture, shipping it back to London. The six-month interval, even with the added responsibility of a sick friend, seemed to him ample. A subject for his picture he hadn't yet chosen. He'd do that, he decided, after some leisurely viewing of the wealth of art, by history's greatest painters, to be seen in Rome's many museums, galleries, churches, and public buildings.

The long weeks spent aboard ship, inevitably, had sobered the excited Severn, opening his eyes to the true nature and extent of the task he'd assumed: the fevered nights, the sudden hard coughing, the sight of blood on the pale lips, alarming even in small quantities, Keats' moody depression lasting hours or days. Especially disturbing were those mysterious "mental sufferings" noted by Severn and that now and again so painfully etched Keats' expressive face, giving rise to that haunted look. To the loyal Severn, the thought that the poet's physical trials were being seriously complicated by something not quite tangible, some lurking harm, was deeply troubling. Whatever was causing the distress, he felt sure, talking about it would help, yet that was the one thing Keats steadily avoided. All during the voyage he'd shown no sign of wanting to unburden himself, no sign that he was yearning for sympathy, making Severn conscious again of the lack of real intimacy between them. But then, only a day after quarantine ended and the ship's party was released to go ashore, Keats suddenly opened his heart, confessing his worries in a rush of naked feeling. For the surprised Severn it proved an unsettling experience, leaving him quite shaken. Clearly, he saw, his function as sole companion was to be far more difficult than he'd ever expected: Keats' silent suffering, it appeared, centered on a badly vexed love affair.

Leaving the brig, the two had been transported by Cotterell to a hotel favored by the English, the Villa da Londra in the Strada di Santa Lucia. At last they could enjoy a good night's rest in a large, well-appointed room affording, as Severn happily noted, a marvelous view of Vesuvius. Next day, November 1st, Keats began a letter to a friend in London (one of his closest, sometime author and man-about-town, Charles Brown), not completing it till evening. Severn, too, that evening sat down to his letter-writing chores, first to his sister—he'd promised his anxious family he'd write first thing—then to a London crony, William Haslam, a young attorney.

With the two bent over their desks, for a while in the room there was only the sharp, edgy sound of scratching quills. Then Keats finished his letter, turned to Severn, and in a confiding tone began to talk. Up to that point in his own letter Severn had been describing Keats' health. Now he interrupted the flow of his thoughts to jot a hasty parenthesis: "(I will talk to him—he is disposed to it—I will talk him to sleep—he has suffered much fatigue)." How long the conversation lasted isn't mentioned. From all indications it was hours. Then Keats, calmer and more rested than he'd felt for a long time, went gratefully to bed.

Next morning as late as 9:30 Keats was still in bed and slumbering peacefully, a fact Severn noted in resuming his letter to Haslam. Their last night's talk, he explained, had turned quite serious, with Keats confessing to some deeply tangled emotions. He'd done his best to comfort the poet, especially concerning "a heavy grief that may tend more than anything to be fatal—he told me much—very much—and I don't know whether it was more painful for me or himself—but it had the effect of much relieving him." Cryptically, he next penned a comment that revealed the strength of his own disturbed response and which must have left Haslam wondering: "If I can but cure his mind I will bring him back to England well—but I fear it can never be done in this world."

Severn's letter to Haslam, a fairly long one recounting incidents of the voyage, is still preserved. It reports in desultory fashion on Keats' condition but supplies no detail of the secret anguish, the "much—very much" disclosed by the agitated poet the previous evening, nothing about the insidious "heavy grief." The ommission is unfortunate, but not crucial, for it is still possible to discover most of what Keats said to Severn that night, to uncover just what that unnamed "grief" was, and to hear it all expressed in Keats' own words. His letter to Brown, finished only minutes before the start of that frank talk, also still survives. A decidedly stark document, it is of prime importance in the looming tragedy. Passing over some incidental remarks, it must be given at nearly its full length:

Naples
Wednesday first in Nov.

My Dear Brown,

Yesterday we were let out of quarantine, during which my health suffered more from bad air and a stifled cabin than it had done the whole voyage. The fresh air revived me a little, and I hope I am well enough this evening to write you a short calm letter—if that can be called one, in which I am afraid to speak of what I would fainest dwell upon. As I have gone thus far into it, I must go on a little—perhaps it will relieve the load of WRETCHEDNESS which presses upon me. The persuasion that I will see Miss Brawne no more will kill me . . .

My dear Brown, I should have had her when I was in health, and I should have remained well. I can bear to die—I cannot bear to leave her. Oh, God! God! God! Everything I have in my trunks that reminds me of her goes through me like a spear. The silk lining she put in my traveling cap scalds my head. My imagination is horribly vivid about her—I see her—I hear her. There is nothing in the world of sufficient interest to divert me from her for a moment . . .

O that I could be buried near where she lives! I am afraid to write to her—to receive a letter from her. To see her handwriting would break my heart—even to hear of her any how, to see her name written would be more than I can bear. My dear Brown, what am I to do? Where can I look for consolation or ease? If I had any chance of recovery, this passion would kill me. Indeed through the whole of my illness, both at your house and at Kentish Town, this fever has never ceased wearing me out . . .

I cannot say a word about Naples, I do not feel at all concerned in the thousand novelties around me. I am afraid to write to her. I should like her to know that I do not forget her. Oh, Brown, I have coals of fire in my breast. It surprises me that the human heart is capable of containing and bearing so much misery. Was I born for this end? . . .

It was obviously in hopes of finding the "consolation" he spoke of, and which at that moment was so badly needed, that the downcast Keats had turned to Severn. He may not, of course, have been as transparent in talking about his feelings for Miss Brawne as he'd been in writing of them. Apparently he came very close to it, for it is plain that Severn was considerably moved by what he heard, for the first time recognizing that his friend's moodiness and disability were not wholly physical. Whether he understood that the wild dejection echoing through the letter to Brown was by no means a thing of the moment, as might seem, the exaggeration of some passing annoyance, is uncertain. Throughout the voyage from England, however, while not mentioned outright, that heavy dejection of spirit had lain as a ponderous weight on Keats' anxious mind, a fact made vividly clear by another letter to Brown, which was then reposing unsent in Keats' trunk. Written at the start of the voyage while the ship lay off Yarmouth, it had not been posted, held back by sudden doubts as to its confessional nature. Had Severn known its contents, with thoughts of death uppermost, he would certainly have felt even greater alarm for his own future and his friend's welfare.

The letter opens with an offhand comment dismissing its seeming low spirits as produced by the frustrations of delay: two weeks of bad weather had blocked the vessel, after leaving London, from getting farther than the Isle of Wight. Nor has he anything very heartening to report about his health, he says, and anyway much prefers just then to avoid topics that are likely to leave him agitated. Yet he couldn't hold himself back, plunging on into the very topic he'd already vowed firmly to shun:

> . . . there is one thing I must mention and have done with it. Even if my body would recover of itself, this would prevent it. The very thing I want most to live for will be a great occasion of my death. I cannot help it . . . were I in health it would make me ill . . . I daresay you will be able to guess on what topic I am harping . . .
>
> I wish for death every day and night to deliver me from these pains, and then I wish death away, for death would destroy even

those pains which are better than nothing . . . death is the great divorcer forever . . .

I think without my mentioning it, for my sake you would be a friend to Miss Brawne when I am dead. You think she has many faults, but for my sake think she has not one—if there is anything you can do for her by word or deed I know you will do it . . .

The thought of leaving Miss Brawne is beyond everything horrible—the sense of darkness coming over me—I eternally see her figure eternally vanishing. Some of the phrases she was in the habit of using during my last nursing at Wentworth Place ring in my ears. Is there another life? Shall I awake and find all this a dream? There must be, we cannot be created for this sort of suffering . . . a sudden stop to my life in the middle of one of these letters would be no bad thing.

Fanny Brawne was well known to Severn. He also knew, as did most of the group of friends, that Keats found her quite attractive—unfortunately so, most felt, for the two didn't seem at all well-suited. What Severn did not know, what very few at the time knew, was that Fanny and Keats were actually engaged to be married. What was understood by no one—Fanny's mother perhaps excepted—was the peculiarly destructive effect of all this on Keats.

Sadly, in the stricken poet's susceptible heart this vivacious young woman had unwittingly set churning a corrosive turmoil of abundant hope, searing doubt, and unquenchable foreboding.

TWO

FANNY

Gazing steadily into her full-length mirror she eyed herself from head to toe. Staring at the piled-up honey-brown hair, her critical inspection dropped slowly down past the bare shoulders, the shapely bosom, the trim waist, the graceful curve of the hips under the long drape of the skirt, to the ruffled hem whose edges brushed the floor. She was quite pleased, she decided at length, with what she saw. She was also, for the thousandth time, more than mildly discouraged and not a little chagrined.

All that the subtleties of dress and grooming could do to bring out or enhance a young woman's physical appeal had been done. All that could be achieved by the even subtler arts of carriage, attitude, and manner to conjure a charm more than physical had been learned— the enticing angle of the creamy shoulders as she turned, the little momentary lift of the chin accompanied by a shy half-smile, so fetching, an unexpectedly glib tongue able to draw and hold attention. But still Fanny Brawne was sadly discouraged. She was eighteen and she was not beautiful.

Staring steadily back at her from the glass, shining with eager intelligence, were two large, pale blue eyes. Wide set, in cast and color it might be said that they were almost pretty. But the remainder of

the face marred the effect, if in a curiously compelling way. A prominent nose—long, narrow, and slightly curving, with a sudden tiny
angle at the midpoint of the arch—rather harshly emphasized the
flat planes of the thin cheeks. Small, pinched nostrils seemed to further constrict the too-narrow mouth, both lips deeply curved, the
pouting lower lip showing much fuller than its partner. The chin,
delicately rounded to a point, served only to complete the impression
of undue length overall. The complexion, though unblemished, was
a shade too dark, almost sallow.

Giving a dismissive wave of her hand she turned away from the
mirror. No, not beautiful. Not even nearly pretty. Plain, to be honest
about it. But what did it really matter! It was all such a game! Men
were so easy to fool in that way, especially young men. At the frequent parties and dances, and those wonderful military balls—with
an army barracks in the area these were rather frequent—there were
always flocks of youthful admirers to tell her how lovely, how ravish-
ing she was. Really, having people—men—*think* you were a scintillating beauty was as good as being one. It was all in how you
managed things. "Dress, manner, and carriage," she once explained
to a correspondent, could quite handily supply the place of physical
attraction. "A person must be a great beauty to look well without
them, but they are certainly within the reach of anybody of understanding."

Fanny at this time, late summer of 1818, lived at home with her
family, a widowed mother, a younger sister (Margaret, aged nine,
who promised to be the real beauty), and a brother Sam, aged fourteen. For years past the Brawnes had occupied a series of rented
houses in Hampstead, an open section of country just northwest of
London. Now as the autumn crowded in they were once again
engaged in the process of packing. All summer they'd rented one half
of a pleasant double house in Hampstead known as Wentworth
Place. Neatly situated, it was well laid out, having two floors and a
lovely back garden (the kitchen and the little dining room being in
the cellar was the only drawback). Best of all, the neighbors in the
other half of the house—Charles Dilke, his wife the pretty Maria,

and his son Charley—had been so very friendly and accommodating, important in such close quarters.

On the day they said goodbye, both Dilkes smilingly insisted that the Brawnes come back to visit often. Their new rental, Elm Cottage, wasn't very far away at all, in fact it was hardly round the corner. So Fanny and her mother, and the children if they liked, mustn't hesitate to make the short walk. A warm welcome would always be waiting, and a nice cup of tea.

The part of Wentworth Place that the Brawnes had rented was owned by Charles Brown, a successful merchant who'd given up business. Of a pronounced literary turn, intent on enjoying life by pleasing himself, he was now a man of independent means and wide London acquaintance who also did some writing. Each year Brown was accustomed to let out his half of the place while he went off on a long holiday. This summer he'd gone roving in the highlands of Scotland with a friend, the young poet John Keats. He'd be returning to take possession of his house in mid-September, so the summer tenants had to be out by then.

During their three months at Wentworth Place the Brawnes had heard much about Keats from the Dilkes, who knew him well and liked and greatly admired him. Charles Dilke too, was a writer, as well as an editor and something of a literary critic. When he talked of Keats he used the most extravagant terms, predicting marvelous things to come. Only twenty-three years old, yet his second volume was even then on sale in the stores. Published the previous April, it was a long verse-narrative called *Endymion*, treating a love story famous in Greek mythology. Of course, in that volume, as well as in the first one, published the year before, there were many faults to be found, along with the good things. But those deficiencies, Dilke was always quick to add, were a mere matter of youthful excess, the raw product of inexperience. It was the sheer *promise* of the performance in *Endymion* that was so marked, unmistakable (four thousand lines of deftly rhyming couplets revealing not only the soul of a gifted poet but nearly a master's touch here and there in prosody and diction). It was what might appear *next* from his pen, that's what everyone was waiting for.

Keats lived with his brother Tom, explained Dilke, in rented rooms in a private house at Well Walk, another village in Hampstead. But often he came over to drop in at Wentworth Place, looking for Brown or himself. Someday soon he hoped to have the pleasure of making the Brawnes and young John acquainted. With everything else, with all his artistic leanings, he was such a downright likeable chap, friendly, talkative, full of good humor, really unstudied. In his finer feelings, though he'd started life as the son of a stablekeeper, he was a true gentleman.

Fanny's first sight of Keats, a casual introduction along with others in the Dilke parlor late in October, left her feeling intrigued, but also a little disappointed. Mr. Keats indeed proved a likeable sort, quite entertaining. Strikingly handsome, too, even with that curiously protruding upper lip that gave his face a slightly pugnacious quality. In the first flush of conversation his sharp intelligence and poetic air were charmingly in evidence. But he was so short! Mr. Dilke hadn't mentioned that. Fanny herself stood a bare five foot three or so, yet when she reached to take the poet's extended hand she had to look down a bit to meet his eyes (those large, lustrous eyes, so fitting for a poet!). She'd never had a personal acquaintance with a man so small and, really, it did take a while to adjust to it.

Over the next week or so the two ran into each other several times at Wentworth Place, and the greetings were always cordial. Somewhat to her surprise, Fanny found that the more time she spent in Mr. Keats' company, the less she thought about his height. The expressive face and the stalwart effect of the upright carriage took your attention, with the result that he actually seemed much taller than he really was. "We met frequently at the home of a mutual friend," Fanny recalled years later when she had settled into life as a wife and a mother, adding that "his conversation was in the highest degree interesting and his spirits good, excepting at moments when anxiety regarding his brother's health dejected them."

The brother, Tom, aged nineteen, had been in failing health for most of the year, from no very definable cause. In the fall he had worsened considerably, and was well and faithfully cared for by John in their cramped, stuffy apartment in Well Walk. By the close of November, when Tom obviously was nearing the end, John scarcely ever left his bedside, the two brothers huddled up together in the smoky, firelit rooms, windows tight shut against the cold and mist.

On December 1st Tom died. The cause was consumption. Unsuspected by anyone, the germs (their existence then unknown to science) coughed out by Tom had found a lodging in Keats' own lungs. For more than a year they would lurk there undetected, quietly waiting in ambush.

※

The first time Keats shook the proffered hand of Fanny Brawne at the Dilke house in October 1818, he felt an immediate strong attraction for what seemed to him a smiling vision of loveliness. In his short life he had already known many young women, sisters of his friends and others, some of them stunning in their fresh beauty. But here was someone not only beautiful but remarkably different, he couldn't think just how. Rather exasperating, too, he had to confess. There were too many moments in company when she'd put herself on display, literally, and proceed to scintillate—nothing less—in word and gesture. That showed a tendency toward a certain kind of social excess that he didn't much care for in any thoughtful, well-brought-up girl, and at some point he'd had the satisfaction of telling her so. Of course, it had made no difference, for she went right on drawing the eyes of all the men in the room her way whenever she felt the urge.

In the middle of December, ten days after Tom's funeral, Keats wrote a long journal-letter to his other brother, George, then an immigrant with his wife and child in America. The writing of it went on at intervals during more than two weeks, and Fanny finds mention in it twice within two days. Together, the passages must have left George wondering. "Mrs. Brawne who took Brown's house for the summer," wrote Keats in the first passage, "still resides in Hampstead. She is a very nice woman and her daughter senior is I think beautiful, elegant, graceful, silly, fashionable and strange. We have a little tiff now and then—and she behaves a little better, or I must have sheered off."

Reading the lines, George would have easily spotted in them his brother's high admiration for the girl, even if it was a puzzled or frustrated sort of liking. It would take a very special kind of woman, George knew, to tie his accomplished brother in such a knot, and as he turned the pages of the letter he was not surprised to come on another bit about Fanny. This passage, much longer and more revealing, appears abruptly in the midst of a running jumble of light-hearted chit-chat, and shows that he has taken particular note of the young lady's behavior, no less than her face and figure. What he says about her face lacking "sentiment" is meant as a compliment, but when he gets to her hands and feet he is talking personal preference. George, himself of average stature, would have understood the reference to Fanny's height as meaning she was a little the taller, which in fact she was:

Shall I give you Miss Brawne? She is about my height with a fine style of countenance of the lengthened sort—she wants sentiment in every feature—she manages to make her hair look well—her nostrils are fine though a little painful—her mouth is bad and good—her Profil is better than her full-face which indeed is not full but pale and thin without showing any bone—her shape is very graceful and so are her movements—Her arms are good her hands badish—her feet tolerable . . .

As he goes on he gets her age wrong (she was a week or two from her eighteenth birthday) and unwittingly reveals his uneasy fascination with the girl's personality, which included a conspicuous lack of reserve in company. Her habit of bestowing nicknames on her

friends uninvited seems to have specially annoyed him, but the interesting question is why he felt himself entitled to speak out, as if chid-
ing her:

> She is not seventeen—but she is ignorant—monstrous in her
> behavior flying out in all directions, calling people such names
> that I was forced lately to make use of the term *Minx*—this I think
> not from any innate vice but from a penchant she has for acting
> stylishly. I am however tired of such style and shall decline any
> more of it.

That made twice in the same week that Keats had complained
about Fanny's atrocious (as he saw it) behavior, and both complaints
had ended with a threat that he'd have nothing more to do with such
an irritating young woman. His objections, if not quite specified, are
boldly stated ("ignorant—monstrous—flying out"). She is at this
time, it appears, one of the crudely insistent sort, interrupting every
conversation with flip opinions and badinage, attempts at wit not
always on the mark or welcome, never lighting for long in one place,
scarcely allowing herself a reflective moment. For Keats, as he said, it
all became merely tiresome.

Piqued by his brother's obviously mixed feelings, the far-off
George would naturally have wanted to hear more, to know how the
little drama was playing itself out. Was his proud, ambitious brother
about to capitulate, to fall victim to the inevitable? How many times
he'd heard John talk earnestly about that, haranguing at length on
the value, indeed the necessity of the single life if an artist were to
accomplish anything worthwhile!

But the sympathetic George was to hear no more about Fanny
Brawne then, and not for a long while after. In another of John's
journal-letters to America, begun in February 1819 and covering
more than two months, Fanny gets only a single short sentence.
Penned in mid-February, the remark comes in abruptly, seeming to
show that little had changed between the two, and that Keats still saw
his new friend as something of a minx: "Miss Brawne and I have

every now and then a chat and a tiff." After that in Keats' letters to his
brother, or to anyone else, there is only silence on the topic of the
enticing Fanny.

At this time in dead earnest about his career as a poet, Keats was
spending at least eight hours a day at his desk, either reading or writing, and by the start of 1819 his focus in study was firmly fixed on
Shakespeare. Thus it was no accident that in one of the lesser-known
plays of his great predecessor he found the perfect literary counter-
part for the infuriating Fanny, a fact of which he soon became acutely
aware. "My greatest torment since I have known you," he told her in a
note some months later, "has been the fear of you being a little
inclined to the Cressid." The notorious flirt, he meant, so starkly
depicted in *Troilus and Cressida*, willful, wayward, shameless Cressida.

Fanny was not at all literary (this she readily admitted, saying she
cared little for poetry aside from one or two of the more exciting bits
in Byron), so she may or may not have understood Keats' bare reference to the play. If not, she would have promptly inquired, and it is
certain she would not have been pleased by what she read, even if she
was able to shrug off Keats' little jab at her as awkward teasing.
Shakespeare's Cressida, a woman both beautiful and witty but artful
and coquettish in the extreme, is the very type and symbol of femi-
nine inconstancy in affairs of the heart, always with strong sexual
overtones.

In the play, a crucial scene has Cressida coyly bantering with a small
group of men, allowing herself to be roundly kissed by each man in
turn. "Fie upon her!" at length blurts one of the men in disgust:

> There's language in her eye, her cheek, her lip;
> Nay, her foot speaks. Her wanton spirits look out
> At every joint and motive of her body.
> O, these encounters so glib of tongue
> That give accosting welcome ere it comes . . .

Young as she was, Fanny knew well the deftly suggestive language of
eyes and lips and each particular part of her own slim-waisted body,

not forgetting the glib tongue. No secret was the cause for all those repeated "tiffs" between her and the poet, or for Keats' own "torment." Yet vow as he might that he'd have nothing more to do with the girl, he found it impossible to forget or ignore her.

Then fate stepped boldly in, circumstances bringing the two of them conveniently together under the same roof.

A few days after Tom's funeral, held on December 7th, Keats left the brothers' Well Walk residence and took up quarters at Wentworth Place as a lodger of Charles Brown. It was a sensible move, suggested by the earnest, empathetic Brown (though Keats paid him the going rate for board and lodging), much better than to have him remain by himself in the doleful quiet of the old apartment with its depressing reminders of poor Tom. Though it wasn't large, Brown's place was well laid out, allowing each man both a bedroom and a private sitting room, for which there was an entrance both outside and inside the house.

Since Fanny was still living with her family at Elm Cottage, distant only a few minutes on foot, the move brought them into close, almost daily contact. Then on April 3rd their meetings were made still more convenient when the Brawnes moved back into Wentworth Place on a long-term lease, occupying the other half of the house, left vacant when the Dilkes moved out to take up residence in the city. The move was decided on by Mrs. Brawne, apparently unaware that between her daughter and Brown's poetic lodger there existed any special attraction.

Before long, though he was then in the throes of composing serious poetry (the much-praised first *Hyperion*, for instance), Keats frequently interrupted himself to rhapsodize about Fanny in verse. The lines he dashed off at this time, mostly of small inspiration, dwell openly on the charm of her physical presence, one sonnet lovingly listing her "Sweet voice, sweet lips, soft hand, and softer breast," not forgetting her "Bright eyes, accomplished shape, and lang'rous waist!" In another sonnet, the well-known "Bright Star," recalling some of their more quietly intimate moments, he pleads in youthful abandon that he might be allowed to shun the world and all its troubles,

> Pillowed upon my fair love's ripening breast,
>   To feel forever its soft fall and swell,
> Awake for ever in a sweet unrest,
>   Still, still to hear her tender-taken breath,
> And so live ever—or else swoon to death.

Another, longer and more intricate poem on Fanny was composed almost immediately after one of their meetings in early April. In it he indulges in a mock complaint that being in love with her, he finds himself no better than a prisoner, bereft even of his poet's power of imagination. What can he do, he asks plaintively, to cancel "remembrance" from his eyes, which scarcely one short hour ago were fixed fascinated on the brilliant Fanny:

> Touch has a memory. O say Love, say,
> What can I do to kill it and be free
> In my old liberty?
> When every fair one that I saw was fair
> Enough to catch me in but half a snare,
> Not keep me there:
> When, howe'er poor and particoloured things,
> My muse had wings . . .

But it is a half-hearted complaint in which he indulges, and he ends by once again gladly surrendering to the vivid memory of their private moments together:

> O, let me once more rest
> My soul upon that dazzling breast!
> Let once again these arms be placed
> The tender jailers of thy waist!

And let me feel that warm breath here and there
To spread a rapture in my very hair . . .

Then as April drew to a close, suddenly, stunningly, from the
scribbling of casual love verse he was swept to an entirely new level of
inspiration, lofty past anything he'd known before—beyond his
years, beyond his knowledge and experience of life, beyond even the
technical artistry he'd shown in his previous writings. In rapid succession he produced four new poems, a ballad and three odes, that
have long since found a place among those very few utterances that
reach to the very pinnacle of lyric poetry. All four were directly
inspired, if on different levels, by his consuming love for Fanny.

The remarkable change that overtook Keats at this time was actually signaled in January, in a lesser way, by his writing of *The Eve of St.
Agnes* (not inspired by Fanny yet surely written as his mind was
aglow with her image). A long verse-narrative telling a simple love
story, it offers little thought or action but much apt description of a
sort that has earned it a special place in the hearts of many readers.
Some weeks later came the ballad, "La Belle Dame Sans Merci," a
short but haunting portrayal of a knight whose heart is mysteriously
entrammeled by a beautiful, enigmatic woman he meets in the
woods (Fanny again). Almost immediately there followed the first of
the three odes, "On a Grecian Urn," then within another few days
came the "To a Nightingale," then "On Melancholy," all finished by
late May.

As with all great art, the three supreme odes have prompted any
number of different, even contradictory interpretations—of course,
as it should be. It is the special genius of poets to say many things at
once, as life itself exhibits not one or two but many interwoven
strands intricately patterned. Yet in pursuing the abstruser meanings
of these three poems, critics seem often to overlook what is surely
their true import and original, underlying inspiration. Each of the
three great odes is a muffled cry from the very depths of the heart
over what appears the cruel transience and shortness of life, and the
heartbreak of its close. Here is a lover—newly minted—in mortal

anguish and despair over the harrowing thought that he, and by extension the woman he loves, will sometime have to die. Momentarily he dreams of alternatives—the seeming permanence to be found in art ("Grecian Urn"), and the soothing absence of individuality among lesser creatures ("Nightingale"). But neither of these ideas, static and lifeless as they are, he finds will serve ("Melancholy"). If being human means eventually to suffer death, it is still far, far better to possess life in all its glorious complexity, freedom, and capacity to feel.

Tragically, after completing the three great odes, Keats was given only another eight months in which to write before illness put a virtual end to his career a full year before his death. In those eight months, still riding the wave of his first inspiration, he wrote many fine things, wonderfully advanced and evocative things, adding to and securing his later fame. But never again, while several times coming close indeed, was he able to attain quite to the lofty height of the three odes. Whatever happened later between him and Fanny Brawne, this must always be remembered in her favor. Keats' love for her, when it was new and vibrant that spring of 1819, gave him the one thing he so greatly craved and in the end was sure he had lost—literary immortality.

In a cottage near the shore, in the small fishing village of Shanklin on the Isle of Wight, Keats sat down to write a letter to Fanny. It was the morning of the first of July 1819, and he had arrived in Shanklin a couple of days before. Now plunged wholeheartedly into a round of serious composition, he needed isolation from all the distractions of the mainland—Fanny herself being not the least of them—as well as a cheap place to live for several months. The cottage he'd found was perfect, nestled at the quiet end of Shanklin's High Street, with windows looking out on rolling green hills while also affording a view of the restless sea. Soon, while inevitably weighed down by thoughts of his absent sweetheart, he reported that he had actually begun to enjoy himself, "wandering as free as a stag about this beautiful Coast."

For this trip he had done some serious planning. Already he had laid out for himself a full, not to say crowded schedule of writing. It was his usual way in composition of overdoing matters, far more than he could reasonably hope to accomplish, including a final polish on some older things to get them ready for book publication. In new composition his main hope was centered on another lengthy verse-narrative he'd been toying with, one he felt had more popular appeal, a colorful tale of a mysterious demom-woman entitled *Lamia* (in this, too, Fanny would make a veiled appearance). Also planned and already begun was an ambitious collaboration with Charles Brown, the two hoping to write a new play to catch the interest of the great Edmund Kean for performance at Drury Lane (a play of Brown's a few years before had had a minor success there, so doors were open). Brown would reach Shanklin in a few weeks. Working together in the same room they hoped to complete the five acts in good time, say a month.

The letter Keats wrote to Fanny that July morning was actually his second attempt in two days. The first he had hesitated to send because it was, as he explained, much too overheated, like one of "those Rhapsodies which I once thought it impossible I should ever give way to, and which I have often laughed at in another." But then, when only halfway through the second letter, he gave way again. It really was too cruel of Fanny, he declares, to have taken his heart captive, in the process destroying his old freedom:

> Will you confess this in a letter you must write immediately and do all you can to console me in it—make it as rich as a draught of poppies to intoxicate me—write the softest words and kiss them that I may at least touch my lips where yours have been. For myself I know not how to express my devotion to so fair a form: I want a brighter word than bright, a fairer word than fair. I almost wish we were butterflies and liv'd but three summer days—three such days

with you I could fill with more delight than fifty common years could ever contain.

The blissful tone, however, then abruptly alters and Keats is heard glumly confessing his old fear that Fanny may not possibly feel the same. For himself, he insists, so far as his own complete happiness is concerned, her love would be more than enough. But "I cannot expect to engross your heart so entirely—indeed if I thought you felt as much for me as I do for you at this moment I do not think I could restrain myself from seeing you again tomorrow for the delight of one embrace. But no—I must live upon hope and Chance."

His apprehension growing, he even allows himself to dwell on the possibility of permanently losing her. Ominously he comments, having in mind no one in particular, "In case of the worst that can happen, I shall still love you—but what hatred shall I have for another!" Ruefully he quotes some lines he had just come across in a play of Massinger's he'd been studying and which had ever since been ringing in his ears, the effect no doubt sharpened by the similarity of names:

> To see those eyes I prize above my own
> Dart favours on another—
> And those sweet lips (yielding immortal nectar)
> Be gently pressed by any but myself—
> Think, think Francesca, what a cursed thing
> It were beyond expression!

Fanny, it appears, had not yet made up her mind about her diminutive poet. Encouragement she certainly gave him, and she seems to have been genuinely attracted, but her heart remained free. She was still young, only eighteen, still learning about men, and this aspiring and rather unsettled young poet was moving much too fast, too furiously. Throughout the affair, up to Keats' departure for Italy two years later, that added fact was in subtle operation, Fanny's uneasy feeling that she was being rushed off her feet. Unfortunately for the sensitive Keats, she went about dealing with her problem in exactly the wrong manner, moved mostly, it seems, by instinct.

Instead of speaking up, of making him understand her wish to go slower, she acted out her message, continuing to indulge her headlong, Cressidish ways. Once she did manage to say something outright, something about its being "not unpleasant to wait a few years" before marriage—surely a broad enough hint. But as will be seen, Keats entirely missed the point. A literary genius he may have been. In the real life of everyday his grasp of nuance and innuendo was often no readier than that of the ordinary young man in love.

One false note he'd already struck, which had begun to trouble Fanny, was his repeated emphasis on her physical allure. This was a topic he would return to endlessly, talking as if she were one of the day's acknowledged great beauties. All too well she knew that she was far from that, and once or twice she'd even asked him not to talk so. A bit chastened, he tried to control himself but couldn't quite manage it, and in a second letter to her from Shanklin, written a week later, he returns clumsily to the subject. This time he can be heard saying precisely the wrong thing.

Speaking not so much as a man in love but more as an enraptured poet in the full glow of composition— a *young* enraptured poet—he actually tells Fanny that it was *only* her beauty that brought him to fall in love with her. "Why may I not speak of your Beauty," he writes, in apparent ignorance of the true effect of what he is saying, "since without that I could never have loved you—I cannot conceive any beginning of such a love as I have for you but Beauty."

Only from what he insists on calling her Beauty with a capital B, her loveliness of face and figure as he sees it, does his love gain "the richness, the bloom, the full form, the enchantment of love after my own heart." Love that proceeds from mere emotional impact, he explains loftily, is nice too, but it's not for him. It was an awkward confession for any young man to have made. Even an authentic beauty would resent and seriously question a love that depended to any extent on such fleeting attractions.

To make matters worse, as Fanny went on reading that second letter she would have found her ardent suitor being woefully inconsistent, demanding for himself the privilege of a directly opposite evaluation. He would not at all appreciate it, he states firmly, if his own growing reputation in literary circles was what attracted her. "I love you the more," he wrote, apparently without thinking, "in that I believe you have liked me for my own sake and for nothing else—I have met with women who I really think would like to be married to a Poem and given away by a Novel." A bright girl, Fanny no doubt caught the glaring contradiction: being loved only for Beauty was no different, no better than being loved only for Genius, and neither would do. That she let Keats' youthful gaffe pass in silence perhaps shows not only that in some ways she was a little the more mature of the two, but felt more for him than he realized.

Keats' letters during this trip went to Fanny faithfully about once a week, and she replied promptly to each. Of her many letters to him none have survived, but stray remarks and comments made in passing by Keats make it possible to hear her voice in the background. Through a close reading of his letters to Fanny, in fact, it is possible to follow the developing affair rather intimately over the course of the next three months, reaching the very day in October when the two became officially engaged—to the surprise and dismay of her own mother and many of their friends, all of whom saw, or thought they saw, a basic incompatability at work between the two.

It is a curious story of love that, on Keats' part, grows until it seems almost overwhelming, is then severely checked and deliberately smothered by him, only to have it again set ablaze by Fanny's physical presence. Not every detail of what happened can be recovered, and this is at least partly because Fanny in later years took pains to destroy several of the more significant letters she received, leaving a gap just at the crucial point. Keats' other letters to Fanny, there are thirty-nine in all, have survived because she carefully preserved them through her remaining forty-five years. She did this initially because they were mementoes of her first tragic love, her lost youth, but at last, as she often told her children, because they would someday "be considered of value."

⁂

Deep at the center of Fanny's personality lay something cold, distant, something that, even when faced with utterly earnest and sympathetic fervor, tempered her response and held her aloof. Keats noticed the cool quality at once but he mistook it for something else, praising it as freedom from the excessively sentimental outlook then fashionable, the melting temperament under strong emotion expected of gentlemen and ladies alike. "She wants sentiment in every feature," he told George approvingly, little realizing what he really saw (once she told a correspondent, "I have no pity whatever for your nerves because I have no nerves"). Now as the summer wore on and letters flew between Wentworth Place and the little Shanklin cottage, he began to suspect something different.

At first, on Keats' part, the rhapsodies continued, to be increasingly well received at the other end. Fanny, like most young ladies, very much enjoyed having impassioned letters addressed to her, the colorful products of a bona-fide poet. In mid-July Keats writes that to him, the mere idea of her love is "touched with ardency," and he says that he slept the night before with her last letter under his pillow (the heat blurred Fanny's initials on the sealing wax and it cost the worried Keats some thought to convince himself that it was not a "bad omen"). He mentions an oriental tale he's been reading, telling of a lovely lady in an enchanted garden who bewitches men, and he adds, "How I applied this to you, my dear; how I palpitated at it." He laments having to "take my candle and retire to a lonely room without the thought as I fall asleep of seeing you tomorrow," then quickly adds that in a month he'll dash up to see her, if only for an hour and even if showing himself to no one else.

A week later he again assures her that "you cannot conceive how I ache to be with you; how I would die for one hour." In her last, Fanny had complained coquettishly that with all his fevered talk of love, he'd taken his good time about declaring himself. In reply, fudging matters a bit, he insists that "I have, believe me, not been an age in letting you take possession of me; the very first week I knew you I wrote myself your vassal, but burnt the letter as the very next time I saw you I thought you manifested some dislike to me." Slyly he adds that if she should ever feel for another man "at first sight what I did for you, I am lost." For the first time he broaches the topic of marriage, bravely stating that while he does not at all look forward to being settled in the world—"I tremble at domestic cares"—yet for Fanny he would gladly assume that burden too. Here again, carried off his feet by the momentum of his racing thoughts, he proceeds to over-reach himself, offering a stark reminder of just how immature in some things he could be, even callow:

> I have two luxuries to brood over in my walks, your loveliness and
> the hour of my death. O that I could have possession of them both
> in the same minute. I hate the world; it batters too much the wings
> of my self-will, and would I could take a sweet poison from your
> lips to send me out of it. From no others would I take it . . . What
> softer words can I find for you after this . . .

Such morbid posturing the practical Fanny could not accept, not even from a poet. Promptly she wrote him so, strongly expressing her displeasure, a fact reflected in the opening sentence of his reply. "You say you must not have any more such letters as the last," he responds lamely. "I'll try that you shall not by running obstinate the other way." Obviously, he'd been stung to think that this teenage girl—no reader of poetry, no delver as he was in philosophy and cosmic imaginings—instead of being impressed by his raw sally had presumed to correct him in what after all was a very crude, very false note.

In this same letter, written in early August, he also forgets to rhapsodize, saying rather flatly that visions of her return to him each night after the "artificial excitement" of a long day spent composing. He repeats his promise to steal up to London for an hour's visit but ends by slightly changing his tune on the subject of domestic cares. Marriage wouldn't be allowed to make *them* staid and stagnant, he insists. *They* wouldn't become those unfortunate sort of people who "wither" at parties, dull dinners, and noisy dances. "No my love, trust yourself to me and I will find you nobler amusements." Since parties, dinners, and dances were the very things Fanny most liked, she wasn't ready to discard them for soberer pastimes. (The grumpy mood stayed with him. In letters to others he dismisses love as "a cloying treacle," and men and women as mere "Shadows").

In the same letter he picked up a remark of Fanny's about having been to a social affair, its nature not specified. Probing, he asks if she is well: "Going out is no proof that you are: How is it? Late hours will do you great harm—what fairing is it?" Where had she been, he is asking, and who with, and he is not at all pleased to hear that it was to a gala officers' ball at the Hampstead barracks ("I am no officer in yawning quarters," he grumbles in his next letter while explaining why his letters have become so "unloverlike").

Together with Brown, Keats was now well into the new play and beginning to feel the need of reference works for background material. On August 12th the two packed up, took the ferry for the mainland, and boarded a stage for Winchester some miles to the north, where there was a good library. Settled into large, pleasant rooms, they prepared for a stay of several weeks, and it was not until the 16th that Keats began another letter to Fanny. Except very briefly at the letter's close, there is nothing in it resembling a young lover's rapture. Instead, running through the casual paragraphs is a clear strain of impatience and subdued complaint.

Because of all the writing he's done in the past six weeks, he apologizes, on *Lamia*, the play, and any number of other things, he can no longer compose overflowing love letters. His brain is "heap'd to the full, stuff'd like a cricket ball," and ready to burst:

> I have had no idle leisure to brood over you—'Tis well perhaps I
> have not—I could not endure the throng of Jealousies that used to
> haunt me before I had plunged so deeply into imaginary inter-

ests ... Give it a fair thinking; and ask yourself whether 'tis not
better to explain my feelings to you, than to write artificial Passion—besides you would see through it—it would be vain to
strive to deceive you . . .

You seem offended at a little simple innocent childish playful-
ness in my last—I did not seriously mean to say that you were
endeavouring to make me keep my promise—I beg your pardon
for it—'Tis but *just* [that] your Pride should take the alarm—*seriously*—You say I may do as I please—I do not think with any conscience I can; my cash-recourses are for the present stopp'd . . .

I am not happy enough for silken Phrases, and silver sentences—I can no more use soothing words to you than if I were at
this moment engaged in a charge of Cavalry—Then you will say I
should not write at all—Should I not?

He closes with a feeble effort at again sounding loverlike—the
thought of Fanny still has power to "uncrystallize and dissolve"
him—and he confesses to more specific memories: "O my love, your
lips are growing sweet again to my fancy—I must forget them."

But his question just before those closing words was plain enough.
Should he continue to write her? Did *she* want his letters to keep
coming? The answer she sent was no doubt a repetition of that care-
less "You may do as you please," quoted by Keats in his letter, meaning, of course, if you do stop writing I'll never speak to you again. So
the letters continued, now passing regularly between Winchester and
Wentworth Place.

Yet it is just here that there occurs that curious gap in the otherwise steady exchange, a lengthy gap of twenty-seven days. The next
letter from Keats to Fanny is dated September 13th and was posted
the following day, not in Winchester but in Lombard Street, London.
A short note, it explains that Keats had come up to the city on some
business for his brother, who had written him from America. He
adds that he will *not* be going the short distance out to Hampstead to
see her, as he'd more than once promised, and will be returning to
Winchester the next morning. The phrasing of the note is hurried

and rather jumbled, requiring some study for full comprehension. But for Fanny one phrase would have needed no analysis: "I have been endeavouring to wean myself from you."

True to his word, Keats avoided Hampstead until he left town the next day. Returning to Winchester, a twelve-hour journey by stage, he plunged immediately back into his writing, principally the play he was doing with Brown. Not for another three weeks did he again see London, arriving back there on October 8th. Whether during that time Fanny and he corresponded can't be said—if they did none of the letters have come to light. His next surviving letter to her is dated October 11th. It was written from London, from entirely new lodgings located at 25 College Street, Westminster.

For a period of fifty-one days, August 16th to October 11th, the only known letter between the two is the brief, disturbing note of September 13th. The full context of his unexpected remark in it about "weaning" himself from Fanny, read even a a dozen times, would have given the puzzled girl little consolation, especially when she found that he'd already been in town for three days without bothering to call:

> I came by the Friday night coach . . . I cannot resolve to mix any pleasure with my days . . . If I were to see you today it would destroy the half comfortable sullenness I enjoy at present . . . I love you too much to venture to Hampstead. I feel it is not paying a visit but venturing into a fire . . . knowing well that my life must be passed in fatigue and trouble, I have been endeavouring to wean myself from you . . . This morning I scarcely know what I am doing . . . I am a Coward, I cannot bear the pain of being happy . . .

On October 8th, when he again returned to London from Winchester, he deliberately reinforced those words, for he purposely avoided going back to his regular rooms at Wentworth Place. Instead, before leaving Winchester he'd asked his friend Dilke, then living in Westminster, to get him a suitable rental in that area. Afterward, for three weeks there is only silence from the College Street lodging, at least no letters from either party have been preserved. Then on October 11th comes another brief note from Keats—and it is enough.

All his resolve about not venturing into a fire has crumbled. On the previous day he had willingly gone up to Hampstead (to fetch some of his things, he may have deceived himself). As his note of the eleventh makes clear, the atmosphere of the meeting with Fanny was very different from the tone of his curt September announcement, in fact quite the opposite. He is still, he sighs, "living today in yesterday," unable to think about or concentrate on anything but her:

> I was in a complete fascination all day. I feel myself at your mercy. Write me ever so few lines and tell me you will never for ever be less kind to me than yesterday . . . You dazzled me . . . When shall we have a day alone? I have had a thousand kisses, for which I thank [you] love—but if you should deny me the thousand and first—'twould put me to the proof how great a misery I could live through . . .

Two days later he is still in a fever over his reawakened hopes, declaring in another letter that the mere thought of her has utterly destroyed his power of writing. "Upon my Soul I can think of nothing else . . . You have ravished me away by a Power I cannot resist, and yet I could resist till I saw you." For the following weekend, October 15th to 17th, he was back again at Wentworth Place, staying in his old rooms in Brown's half of the house, a step away from Fanny in the other half. Of this interlude, how they spent the time together, no actual record remains. Yet Keats' own later succinct description of it is perhaps sufficient. "My three days dream," he fondly remembered it while quoting an appropriate line from *The Tempest*, "I cry to dream again!"

One immediate result of that October visit is definitely known, the fact that Keats decided to move himself back to his rooms in Wentworth Place. Another result, more crucial yet hardly surprising in the circumstances, yields to close study of all the sources. No longer deterred by the threat of domestic cares and dinner invitations, Keats had asked for Fanny's hand and had gotten it. The two were now officially engaged to be married.

A third fact, not a little troubling as a sign of what was to come, is also readily discovered: Fanny's continuing childish tendency to tease her fiancé with her airy attitude and loose, flirting habits. In each of Keats' three October letters to her he brings up her supposedly lighthearted joking on the matter, leaving little doubt that he considered such behavior to be decidedly unfunny.

On the twelfth he warns Fanny that his heart, not his vanity or pride, would be hurt, "If you should ever carry your threat yesterday into execution."

On the thirteenth he asks plaintively, "My sweet Fanny, will your heart never change? My love, will it? . . . Do not threat me even in jest."

On the nineteenth, with the engagement only a week old, his tone becomes markedly sober, and he comments abruptly, "If you ever intend to be cruel to me as you say in jest now but perhaps may sometime be in earnest; be so now."

Cressida indeed, and no allowance made for the nervously playful spirit of an intelligent, in some ways accomplished, but very young woman who was still all too unsure of herself and her appeal.

THREE

LOVE IS NOT A PLAYTHING!

When the stagecoach for Hampstead left London at 10:30 on the night of February 3, 1820, Keats was among its passengers. Occupying one of the cheaper outside seats atop the swaying vehicle in order to save money, he shivered through the half-hour trip. Deceived that morning by a sudden spell of mild weather after a cold, snowy January, he'd left his overcoat at home. Now even with the wide collar of his jacket pulled tight up around his ears he felt the sharp bite of the rushing wind.

Money, in the form of an assured and steady income, had indeed at this time become a troubling question in Keats' mind. As a single man consumed by dreams of a literary career, fittingly disdainful of crasser matters, he'd never given more than a passing thought to the topic of finances. Now that love and his hopes of a speedy marriage had driven even poetry into the background, he was faced with the urgent need to make a decision. Go back to medicine? With his training it would be easy to find a spot as an apothecary (then much more than a mere chemist, in fact almost a doctor). Become a journalist writing essays for one of the newer London periodicals? Already he'd done some of that, and with his name now known fairly well in literary circles it should be no problem to catch on somewhere as a critic or commentator. What else? A regular business of some sort, get into some firm through his various contacts in the city (the thought brought on a slight shuddering unrelated to the cold breeze). All he needed was an income sufficient to allow Fanny and himself to continue living on a comfortable level, naturally with some provision for the future.

The Brawnes had money, he knew, and Fanny when she came of age would get her part of the family inheritance, no fortune but a satisfying little pile. He'd never touch a shilling of that, of course. But it meant that Fanny, already accustomed to a certain degree of affluence, could reasonably expect the same in her marriage. No bare rooms or windowless curtains for her, no servantless kitchen or sitting dutifully every night tending the fire. How he'd be able to fit his own writing into all this he wasn't quite sure—*that* was the question! His writing had already suffered, in fact, all but collapsing for the past few months. As well as rewriting older things he'd worked on a number of new poems but had felt woefully little inspiration or satisfaction. No spark. He wasn't sure why. Maybe just a dry spell. (Some things *had* pleased him, for instance parts of the revamped *Hyperion*, which he thought really quite good).

Still, he was in love and Fanny was his! Soon they'd be joined forever, settled together somewhere, and then his accustomed overflowing imagination would come back and he'd be writing again in his old abundant, carefree way, and they'd be staring at a future glowing with felicity and promise.

The rumbling stage was now almost to Hampstead. On his high perch the shivering poet, thankful that the journey was nearly ended, listened absently to the rapid clop-clopping of the horses' hooves in the darkness. Suddenly he felt something in his chest, an uneasiness, a tightness, and he was aware that his breathing had become labored. With alarm, he felt his lungs growing warm, as if filling with hot liquid. Moments later he began coughing, a harsh, wracking cough, and some of the warm, thick liquid rose in his windpipe, spilling into his mouth. Blood, he thought as he spat over the side of the stage, blood! He could taste it. Blood!

For some seconds the heated sensation in his chest continued, while at the same time his breathing became increasingly difficult, and then he found himself gasping. Holding on frantically to the side railing, he began to feel as if he would not survive the sudden attack another second. Trying to cough, his eyes rolling in his head, he waited to black out, to pitch headlong to the fast-rushing ground. But in that wild instant, instead of panic, he felt only a curious calm, seeing only the face of the lovely Fanny. "On the night I was taken ill," he told her later, "when so violent a rush of blood came to my lungs that I nearly suffocated—I assure you I felt it possible I might not survive and at that moment thought of nothing but you."

Abruptly the severity of the attack began to ease, and he found that he could breathe again without distress. At Pond Street, the stage stop in Hampstead, he was recovered sufficiently to climb down unaided. Wentworth Place wasn't far from Pond, ordinarily a walk of some five minutes. Now to Keats, breathing easier but feeling flushed and weak, his legs trembling, it seemed interminable miles away.

Brown was at home that night and when Keats entered the front door happened to be in the parlor. What he saw shocked him: "At eleven o'clock he came into the house in a state that looked like fierce intoxication. Such a state in him, I knew, was impossible; it therefore was the more fearful." Anxiously Brown asked what was the matter, was he fevered? "Yes, yes," answered Keats, "I was on the outside of the stage . . . severely chilled, but now I don't feel it. Fevered! Of course, a little." Readily he accepted Brown's urging that he go straight up to bed.

As Keats mounted the stairs, Brown lit a candle and hurried off to get some brandy. When he reached Keats' room some moments later the undressed poet, shrinking at the touch of the cold sheets, was just climbing into bed. His head sinking wearily toward the pillow, he broke into a cough and from his contorted lips there spewed a small quantity of warm liquid. Blood again. He bent close, peering anxiously at one large drop. "Bring me the candle," he murmured, "Let me see the colour of this blood."

The small flame cast a flickering patch of yellow on the white

sheet, making the blood spot gleam a bright red. Silent and unmoving, his narrowed eyes inches from the stain, Keats stared steadily, his
brain crowded by stark visions of all the flowing or smeared blood
he'd seen and felt as a medical student. Then he turned his head,
looked up at the hovering Brown, and "with a calmness of countenance" that Brown could never forget, voiced the worst possible
interpretation of what had happened. "This is unfortunate," said
Keats in an even tone, " . . . I know the colour of that blood. It's arte-
rial blood . . . that drop is my death-warrant." Thinking of his
mother and brother before him, he was sure on the instant that he'd
been stricken by the terror of consumption.

Staggered by his friend's pronouncement—so calmly delivered as
it was, and coming from a qualified apothecary—Brown watched as
Keats stretched himself on the bed, then said he'd run down the
street and fetch Dr. Rodd, a physician well known in the neighborhood. Alone in the candlelit room, Keats lay nervously waiting his
friend's return, and soon he heard the men bustling in at the front
door. Making only a brief examination, Dr. Rodd promptly decided
that his patient must be bled (the day's universal first remedy, no
matter the diagnosis, and in this case, in light of later knowledge,
precisely the wrong action). By midnight the bleeding was finished
and Keats seemed dozing off. With that the doctor left, first saying
he'd like to call in a London specialist, Dr. Bree, an authority on res-
piratory diseases. The young man's symptoms, he explained, so far as
he could determine, did not unerringly point to consumption. The
trouble might well be something else entirely.

Not until he made his second or third call at Wentworth Place
some two weeks after the attack did Dr. Bree feel ready to supply a
definite diagnosis. The disease wasn't in the lungs, he said, nothing
like that: Mr. Keats had "no pulmonary affection, no organic defect
whatever." The trouble had arisen wholly from "his *Mind*." Here was
a clear case of too much mental exertion too long sustained, brought
to a head by exposure on that stage ride from London. Too much
reading, too much writing, too much mental and of course emotional embroilment of all sorts. Probably the doctor had learned of

the huge pile of original writing Keats had turned out in the previous year—poem after poem, one after another without letup, long poems and short, their composition often overlapping, then a five-act play done in collaboration in barely a month, while at the same time tossing off big chunks of the lengthy and demanding *Lamia*! Even a young mind, strong as it might be, couldn't go on like that without risking a weakened constitution, Dr. Bree explained, thus becoming a prey to the first untoward circumstance.

The hemorrhage had obviously been caused by the severe chill he'd caught that night, in cold weather made much worse by the piercing wind howling against the racing vehicle. If he'd taken an inside seat it's likely that none of this would have happened.

A complete cure could be expected, and the way was simple. First, *rest*, plenty of rest. No physical exertion. No excitement. No writing of any sort, especially no writing of poetry. No *reading* of poetry, either. A restricted vegetarian diet would be a great help, and it would also be better if fewer of his friends came to call (there had been a steady parade of them, the women bringing him enough jars of jams and jellies to stock a store). His special friend from the other side of the building might call occasionally, but she must be calm and quiet, and must not remain long.

There was no medication available that would be specially efficacious, only laudanum (a mixture of alcohol and opium). Some of that would relax him, help to settle him down. Should he grow nervous or fidgety, or find himself unable to sleep, he could send round to the chemist for a bottle or two. The dosage and its frequency would depend on how he felt.

All this was very good news indeed, and Keats duly passed the welcome verdict on to his sister: "The Doctor tells me there are no dangerous Symptoms about me and that quietness of mind and fine weather will restore me." Another note to his sister expands a bit on that bare statement, giving some specifics of his ailment and its cause, as diagnosed by the physician: "The doctor assures me that there is nothing the matter with me except nervous irritability and a general weakness of the whole system which has proceeded from my anxiety of mind of late years and the too great excitement of poetry." His sister would have understood more by those few words than today appears to a casual reading. Her brother was assuring her that the dreaded consumption was not in question, that he would not be leaving her to go the way of poor Tom.

Privately, though, there were moments when he had his doubts that it could be that simple, when he still worried that there might be "something wrong about me which my constitution will either conquer or give way to." In any case, the prescription for rest did not include staying in bed the whole day, and he was soon taking regular strolls round the back garden, fifteen minutes, then a half-hour at a time. A slight setback occurred early in March when he was taken one evening with rather violent heart palpitations. But Dr. Bree, hurriedly summoned, found little cause for worry, pronouncing his patient quite unaffected by the incident. By the last days of March Keats felt so far recovered, so fit and energetic, that he went down to London where he spent an afternoon viewing a friend's painting on exhibition in Egyptian Hall (B. R. Haydon's *Christ's Entry into Jerusalem*, in which Keats' head appears as one of the crowd).

His fear of consumption had now receded until it was no more than the dull twinge at the back of his mind it had long been.

The slow-dragging days of his convalescence during February and March had been made much more bearable by the almost daily presence of Fanny. If she was not beside him in the parlor, then she was tapping at his window, or waving to him from the back garden, or was heard as a familiar voice or footstep when she left the house or returned. Her teasing ways about the attentions she received from other men, her "jesting" about being "cruel" to him, were ended, finished for good, as she said. Now she was his one unfailing source of healing balm for a vexed spirit, with its inevitable restorative effect on the ailing body.

While he convalesced, the two wrote each other encouraging little notes, more than twenty of which have survived (only his, none of hers). In the first of these, written a day or so after the attack, he assures her that "the consciousness that you love me will make a pleasant prison of the house next to yours. You must come and see me frequently: this evening without fail." A few days later he writes that he is eagerly looking forward to "Health and the Spring and a regular routine of our old walks." Just discernible in the veiled language of the notes, before he'd been given Dr. Bree's reassuring verdict, is his fleeting thought that he should release Fanny from her promise. As a struggling poet stricken with ill health, perhaps even the doom of consumption, he decided he had no right to hold her. His offer of release was made to the girl about mid-February. In return he was given a prompt and apparently indignant refusal by the surprised young woman. "How hurt I should have been," he wrote her that night, "had you ever acceded to what is, notwithstanding, very reasonable! How much the more do I love you from the general result!"

Feeling reassured, he even grew more tolerant of Fanny's liking for social life, encouraging her to find some relief from attending on him, for instance to resume her visits to friends in the city for parties and dances. "Let me not longer detain you from going to Town," he urged. "There may be no end to this imprisoning of you." Gladly she took him up on the suggestion, accepting several invitations, though prudently refusing some others, at the same time making sure to let her fiancé know of this commendable restraint. His own answering comment, just a bit labored, gave assurance that, while he was much gratified "by your remaining at home," he did not at all mind "you going to Town . . . though I am pleased with the one, I am not displeased with the other." Carried away, he said he could envision her at home "sitting in your new black dress which I like so much." It made an enticing picture, and he said he could hardly keep from running around to "surprise you" with a knock at the door.

By the beginning of March he was able to manage one of his old, overflowing love letters, working himself up to the sort of emotional pitch the doctors had warned him against:

My Dear Girl I love you ever and without reserve. The more I have known you the more have I lov'd. In every way—even my jealousies have been agonies of Love, in the hottest fit I ever had I would have died for you . . .

The last of your kisses was ever the sweetest; the last smile the brightest; the last movement the gracefullest. When you passed my window home yesterday I was filled with as much admiration as if I had then seen you for the first time. You uttered a half complaint once that I only lov'd your Beauty. Have I nothing else then to love in you but that? Do not I see a heart naturally furnished with wings imprison itself with me? No ill prospect has been able to turn your thoughts a moment from me . . .

Even if you did not love me I could not help an entire devotion to you: how much more deeply then must I feel for you knowing you love me. My Mind has been the most discontented one that ever was put into a body too small for it. I never felt my Mind repose upon anything with complete and undistracted enjoyment—upon no person but you. When you are in the room my thoughts never fly out the window: you always concentrate my whole senses. The anxiety shown about our Loves in your last note is an immense pleasure to me . . .

April saw the culmination of Keats' recovery, his old energy restored, his smiling face filled out from its slight emaciation, his usual upright bearing and swinging stride again conspicuous. The improvement was so marked that when Brown announced his plan for another walking tour of Scotland, Dr. Rodd agreed, in fact urged, that Keats should go along if only for the boat journey north— leisurely days spent in the bracing air of a sailing vessel, then strolling through the Highlands, just the thing! Keats himself, with Brown's reluctant concurrence, decided against it. The sensible suggestion was also made by someone, the doctor or one of Keats' friends, that he might think about spending the following winter in Italy, as so many were doing with great benefit. Keats didn't like that idea at all, and anyway doubted that he could find the money for it.

Brown's departure brought another sort of disruption for Keats, the need to find himself a lodging for the summer. As usual when Brown went off for one of his lengthy holidays, his portion of Wentworth Place had been rented. For four months, May through August, Keats would need to reside elsewhere, returning to live at Wentworth Place only in September. Something suitable might have been found in Hampstead, no doubt, allowing him to remain near Fanny. Yet he elected to move some two miles away, taking rooms in the tidy little village of Kentish Town. Since his old friend and early encourager, Leigh Hunt, lived there, no mystery attaches to his choice. Writer, editor, poet, and a man who had his pulse on literary London, Hunt was just the man to steer Keats in his fast-rising hopes of breaking into periodical writing. The two miles that lay between him and Fanny were really nothing for a man in good health, easily covered on foot in a brisk twenty minutes. On May 4th he moved his little store of belongings to the new place. Two days later he took his temporary leave of Fanny.

With that parting, quite abruptly, a curtain descends on the scene, blotting out all knowledge of the events of the next two or three weeks. Whatever happened during that time between the two, when the curtain again goes up it is seen that a radical change has occurred.

For the poet, alone in his Kentish Town rooms with little to occupy him (his only necessary task was the correction of proofs for his new volume of poetry, due in June), Fanny is no longer the object of his uncritical devotion. No longer is she the "undistracted enjoyment" he'd named her in a letter scarcely a month earlier. Instead, his tone angry past anything he'd penned before, she is now railed at by her despairing lover as cruel and heartless, the cause of endless, excruciating "torments."

The six letters that Keats wrote to Fanny during his three-month stay in Kentish Town in the summer of 1820 were published only in 1878, along with all his other letters to her. Immediately, three of the six became the storm center of Keats biography, and have remained so ever since. In view of the tangle that has resulted from that heated debate during more than a century (one respected scholar didn't hesitate to charge that Fanny "killed" her lover), a more searching look at those letters, already among the most studied documents in literary history, is in order. For that purpose, of course, the letters themselves must be placed in evidence, and at their full length or almost. Though each of the three is rather long, they will not weary any reader curious to see into the still-youthful heart of a poet who lived as much in his own restless, roving mind as he did in the world.*

When leaving Wentworth Place on May 6th, Keats was in a good mood, though still being careful to avoid excitement, as the doctor had directed. "I am afraid to ruminate on anything which has the shade of difficulty or melancholy in it," he told his sister, "since that sort of cogitation is so pernicious to health." To Charles Brown, some two weeks after that, he reported that he was "very well," and added that he expected to get "more pleasure than pain out of the summer." Settling in Kentish Town, he passed the time with visits to Hunt's house which stood a few doors away, seeing other friends at his own place or in the city, and working at the proofs of his book. He also sneaked in a little work on some new writing, nothing too demanding.

A full month passed, quite a pleasant month so far as is known. Under orders to get as much fresh air as possible, on the morning of June 14th he left his rooms for his usual stroll round the neighborhood. Returning before noon he sat down and reached for his pen:

> My Dearest Girl,
>   I have been a walk this morning with a book in my hand, but as usual I have been occupied with nothing but you: I wish I could

---

*The true sequence and exact dating of the three letters continues in doubt, though not the fact that they were written from Kentish Town in May–July 1820. My own view of the question is fully discussed in the Notes. The originals are all unparagraphed, Keats' usual way. Breaking them up a bit, as here, I feel is permissible as an aid to readier comprehension.

say in an agreeable manner. I am tormented day and night. They talk of my going to Italy. 'Tis certain I shall never recover if I am to be so long separate from you: yet with all this devotion to you I cannot persuade myself into any confidence of you. Past experience connected with the fact of my long separation from you gives me agonies which are scarcely to be talked of. When your mother comes I shall be very sudden and expert in asking her whether you have been to Mrs. Dilke's, for she might say no to make me easy.*

I am literally worn to death, which seems my only recourse. I cannot forget what has pass'd. What? nothing with a man of the world, but to me deathful. I will get rid of this as much as possible. When you were in the habit of flirting with Brown you would have left off, could your own heart have felt one half of one pang mine did. Brown is a good sort of Man—he did not know he was doing me to death by inches. I feel the effect of every one of those hours in my side now; and for that cause, though he has done me many services, though I know his love and friendship for me, though at this moment I should be without pence were it not for his assistance, I will never see or speak to him until we are both old men, if we are to be. I *will* resent my heart having been made a football. You will call this madness.

I have heard you say it is not unpleasant to wait a few years— you have amusements—your mind is away—you have not brooded over one idea as I have, and how should you? You are to me an object intensely desirable—the air I breathe in a room empty of you is unhealthy. I am not the same to you—no—you can wait—you have a thousand activities—you can be happy without me. Any party, anything to fill up the day has been enough.

How have you pass'd this month? Who have you smil'd with? All this may seem savage in me. You do not feel as I do—you do not know what it is to love—one day you may—your time is not

---

*The Dilkes, for Fanny an active social outlet, were then settled in the heart of London.

come. Ask yourself how many unhappy hours Keats has caused you in Loneliness. For myself I have been a Martyr the whole time, and for this reason I speak; the confession is forc'd from me by the torture. I appeal to you by the blood of that Christ you believe in: Do not write to me if you have done anything this month which it would have pained me to have seen. You may have altered—if you have not—if you still behave in dancing rooms and other societies as I have seen you—I do not want to live—if you have done so I wish this coming night may be my last.

I cannot live without you, and not only you but *chaste you; virtuous you.* The Sun rises and sets, the day passes, and you follow the bent of your inclination to a certain extent—you have no conception of the quantity of miserable feeling that passes through me in a day. Be serious! Love is not a plaything—and again do not write me unless you can do it with a crystal conscience. I would sooner die for want of you than—*

> Yours for ever
> J. Keats

What on earth has happened? What has triggered this frantic outcry against the girl he loves, all this piercing doubt? The known record gives no hint, so the letter itself is the only hope. As it turns out, close study does indeed supply an answer, one which simple reason goes far to make certain.

He has heard something. From some friend or acquaintance, met in Kentish Town or London, he has learned some fact about Fanny and her old, loose ways, something he can't help believing. The report need not have been malicious or unkind, might have been told him in a jocular fashion, might have come from someone who knew little or nothing of his special ties to the girl. But he must have heard *something.* To conclude otherwise, to say that the letter with its searing accusation was written without the least real provocation,

---

*The implied conclusion of the sentence is obvious—and telling: "than have to share you with other men."

prompted by nothing more than the poet's own lonely brooding (the theory generally preferred today) is to confess its writer as being seriously unbalanced. Psychotic is the word.

Some degree of clinical depression, in fact, is now generally if reluctantly conceded, especially by Fanny's defenders. One biographer, Amy Lowell, was sure that Keats had lost himself in "delirium" and gone "temporarily mad." Another, the more judicious Aileen Ward, felt that there had been a "poisonous effect" on Keats' overworked mind caused by "isolation from Fanny." Still another, the meticulous Robert Gittings, found that Keats' mental outlook had been badly eroded, "slowly darkened in solitude," bringing back what he calls the poet's "deep-rooted distrust of women." W. J. Bate, still after more than thirty years perhaps Keats' most respected biographer, was sure that "inevitably" the poet in his loneliness simply lost his bearings "when he began to picture Fanny . . . enjoying herself in the company of other people."

True, the letter is vehement, passionate to excess, savage even. Yet in tone it is controlled, doesn't ramble or meander, makes direct, sharp, specific points. Beneath the violent phrases it gives quite a rational impression, and other letters written to other people at the time show him very much in his usual frame of mind. Surely the letter's impetus, its reckless driving pace, arose from some infuriating tale about Fanny, one that carried its own guarantee of authenticity (proof is found in the second letter, though lacking details). Certainly it would have involved her being seen in the company of another man or men, gayly accepting or inviting their attentions—those "encounters so glib of tongue," as Shakespeare wrote of Cressida, "that give accosting welcome ere it comes."

Added to the original anger, it may be admitted, increasing the force of the explosion, were some underlying factors, dimly realized. Doubt and discouragement over his physical stature was always present, and nagging fears as to his health. Now at the back of his mind grimly sat the awful idea that he might die before completing at least the one long poem or play needed to prove his worth. Beyond that there may have been, probably was in some degree, his intense if

unspoken desire to see embodied in Fanny some pure ideal of
abstract beauty—pernicious factor indeed, able to vex and trammel
almost any love affair.

The picture painted in Keats' all-too-receptive mind by the story
he'd heard, whatever it was, brought rushing back similar complaints
of the previous year, now including the surely innocent Brown himself.
"You will call this madness," says Keats defensively about the Brown
charge, showing his own doubt in the matter. Inescapably, he then
becomes alarmed at the possibility on Fanny's part of more recent mis-
behavior, now, as he perhaps concludes, encouraged by his absence.

"How have you passed this month?" he demands as if by right,
"who have you smil'd with? . . . Do not write me if you have done
anything this month . . . " Was she still making a vulgar display of
herself in dancing rooms and at parties, "as I have seen you"? The
phrase in itself tells much. Were it not true—implying several such
sightings, not just one—he could not have used it in writing Fanny.
At bottom, also, and all too clearly, his jealousy was largely of a sexual
nature, and thus all the wilder. If Fanny kissed and petted with *him* as
she did (on the evidence, there is no question of more than that),
what was to prevent her from allowing the same privileges elsewhere?
If the fact of her being an engaged woman failed to halt her habitual,
indiscriminate flirting, where *would* it stop?

With the letter finished, he didn't post it. Reading it over, he at last
felt the full impact of its brutal excess, making him hesitate. Folding
it, he let it sit overnight on his desk. Next morning he took up his pen
to try again, thinking to write something calmer. But as he traced the
first sentence on the thin paper all his bitterness of the previous day
again welled up:

My Dearest Girl,

I wrote a Letter for you yesterday expecting to have seen your
mother. I shall be selfish enough to send it though I know it may
give you a little pain, because I wish you to see how unhappy I am
for love of you, and endeavour as much as I can to entice you to
give up your whole heart to me whose whole existence hangs upon

you. You could not step or move an eyelid but it would shoot to my heart—I am greedy of you—Do not think of anything but me. Do not live as if I was not existing—Do not forget me—

But have I any right to say you forget me? Perhaps you think of me all day. Have I any right to wish you to be unhappy for me? You would forgive me for wishing it, if you knew the extreme passion I have that you should love me—and for you to love me as I do you, you must think of no one but me, much less write that sentence.

Yesterday and this morning I have been haunted with a sweet vision—I have seen you the whole time on your shepherdess dress. How my senses have ached at it! How my heart has been devoted to it! How my eyes have been full of Tears at it! Indeed I think a real Love is enough to occupy the widest heart—

Your going to town alone, when I heard of it, was a shock to me—yet I expected it—*promise me you will not for some time, till I get better.* Promise me this and fill the paper full of the most endearing names. If you cannot do so with a good will, do my Love tell me—say what you think—confess if your heart is too much fasten'd on the world. Perhaps then I may see you at a greater distance, I may not be able to appropriate you so closely to myself. Were you to lose a favorite bird from the cage, how would your eyes ache after it as long as it was in sight; when out of sight you would recover a little.

Perhaps if you would, if so it is, confess to me how many things are necessary to you besides me, I might be happier, by being less tantaliz'd. Well may you exclaim, how selfish, how cruel, not to let me enjoy my youth! to wish me to be unhappy! You must be so if you love me—upon my Soul I can be contented with nothing else. If you could really what is called enjoy yourself at a party—if you can smile in peoples faces, and wish them to admire you *now*, you never have nor ever will love me—

I see *life* in nothing but the certainty of your Love—convince me of it my sweetest. If I am not somehow convinced I shall die of agony. If we love we must not live as other men and women do—I cannot brook the wolfsbane of fashion and foppery and tattle. You must be mine to die upon the rack if I want you.

I do not pretend to say I have more feeling than my fellows—but I wish you seriously to look over my letters kind and unkind and consider whether the Person who wrote them can be able to endure much longer the agonies and uncertainties which you are so peculiarly made to create—My recovery of bodily health will be of no benefit to me if you are not all mine when I am well. For god's sake save me—or tell me my passion is too awful a nature for you. Again God bless you.

J. K.

No—my sweet Fanny—I am wrong. I do not want you to be unhappy—and yet I do, I must while there is so sweet a Beauty—my loveliest my darling! Good bye! I kiss you—O the torments!

The first paragraph tells it all. The story he'd heard about Fanny was the last straw ("a shock to me"). Engaged to him as she was, her lighthearted career of emotional sauntering must cease: "Give up your *whole* heart to me . . . *Think* of no one but me." The rest of the letter, behind its tumultuous air, only adds to that note. There is to be no more going to town alone, no unchaperoned parties or dances or desultory visits, making her fair game for every wandering male attracted by that enticing smile. Her cute way of hinting about all the attention she received from other men must also stop: "You must think of no one but me," he insists, "much less write that sentence." If all this seemed selfish, too soon curtailing her freedom, so be it. "I can be contented with nothing else. . . . convince me." The endearments he sprinkles through the postscript are barely enough to mute his final warning that he can no longer live with those agonies of spirit "you are so peculiarly made to create."

Then, again, he goes too far. His poet's heart groping for some image or graphic phrase to enforce his meaning, before he is fully aware of what he is writing, he scribbles, "You must be mine to die upon the rack if I want you." Even for hyperbole that is more than a little over the line. But it makes its point. If such entire loyalty is beyond her, then "*tell* me my passion is too awful." All or nothing.

Painfully evident also in the letter—though it needs close attention to spot it in the rush of feeling—is Keats' own halting realization that he is going too far. At the letter's midpoint (paragraphs four and five) he makes a fleeting and stumbling effort to appear reasonable, inviting Fanny to state plainly whether she *must* have the society of other people "besides me," the comfort of other "things." In that case, he declares, he might begin to feel easier, not be so disturbingly "tantaliz'd" by uncertainty. But no sooner are the words inked on the paper than he reverses himself. If she *does* require the stimulus of other people in her life, he announces, then she's not the girl for him. Three short sentences after that he falls headlong into the crudity of his remark about Fanny dying on the rack.

By June 16th, or at most within a day or two afterward, Fanny held in her hand an envelope bearing her name in Keats handwriting, its bulk a bit thicker than usual. It would not have mattered which of the two letters she read first (neither bears a date), since their rude impact would have been about equal. How long she required to get over her surprise and the resentment that surely followed, and pen her answer, and just what she may have written are tantalizing questions now past resolving with precision. But it is known that she did reply, by letter, and certainly within a day or two. On good evidence—a later, fairly explicit letter of his to her, to be quoted from shortly—much of what she said can also be recovered. (With all the uniqueness of these two, how their troubled exchange still echoes what has so often been said since time began between ardent young lovers!)

Admitting no fault, making no apologies, she complained that he had terribly wronged her, "in thought, word, and deed." Whatever he has heard, she is not the sort of empty-headed female he seemed to think. When enjoying herself among her friends, did he really expect her to sit stony-faced in a corner? At twenty must she act the matron when young men crowded up to speak with her?

Anyway, she's had to put up with a lot, too, those so-called friends of his who went around laughing at her as not good enough for him,

saying that he should have a wife of some breeding and sophistica-
tion, a woman of more mature intellect, able to understand his artistic ambitions and appreciate those wonderful poems. He needn't
think she didn't know about the hateful things they were saying,
making her out not only shameless but a dolt and a ninny as well.
Easy to see who *he's* been listening to!

Just what did he mean she asked, about seeing her "at a greater
distance," and not holding her "so closely"? What did he mean about
being satisfied "with nothing else," and insisting that she "convince"
him? Was he trying to say he'd like to break the engagement? Is that
what he meant about her interests being "too much fasten'd on the
world'? Maybe she really *wasn't* good enough for him! But even after
those two horrid letters he'd written she wanted him to know that
she *did* love him and would always be his, "heart and soul," if he
wanted her.

Having written and posted her reply, Fanny waited anxiously for
an answer, perhaps even anticipating a flying visit from her agitated
fiancé. A full week later, however, neither letter nor fiancé had
appeared at Wentworth Place. Another day or two went by, and then
Fanny knew the reason why there had been nothing but silence. On
June 22nd disaster had struck again.

That morning early, Keats had left his rooms to make a visit to his
sister at her guardian's home in Walthamstow. Hardly had he started
along the street when a slight cough made him halt, and he brought
up a small quantity of blood, little more than a few specks and
smears but enough to frighten him. Returning to the house he waited
in some apprehension, but nothing further happened. Later that day,
breathing freely and with none of the old tightness in his chest, he
felt entirely fit again, his reawakened fears fast receding.

Earlier, he'd accepted a dinner invitation from Hunt, and that
evening he walked the few steps over to the Hunt residence in
Mortimer Terrace, where he was intoduced to Hunt's other guests,
Mr. and Mrs. Gisborne, friends of Shelley. In her diary, Mrs.
Gisborne next day noted with interest how she'd met the young
author of *Endymion*, parts of which had so impressed Shelley. Then

she added that, disappointingly, during the whole evening Keats "spoke but little," and when he did say something it was always delivered "in a low tone."

Strikingly, if unwittingly, that diary entry provides a miniature sketch of the poet, depressed and physically languid, as he was about to suffer another serious hemorrhage. It happened later that same evening when he was alone in his rooms, an hour or two after he'd said goodbye at Hunt's.

No question about it, declared Dr. Lambe, Mr. Keats must go to Italy for the winter. Whether the complaint was indeed full-blown consumption, no one could tell just then. The bleeding and the fever were as likely to be caused by any number of other things, bad heart or stomach, excessive fatigue, overwork, mental perturbation, coughing from a severe chill that ruptured a blood vessel. But it might well be the start of phthisis, and even if it should prove otherwise, the warm south was the very place to fight constitutional debilitation. Specialist Dr. Robert Darling, who'd already been to Mortimer Terrace to consult on the case, was in full agreement. Mr. Keats really should be on his way no later than early September. A couple of months in which to make his arrangements wasn't much time, considering the slowness of the mails down through France and across the Alps.

The unwelcome verdict was delivered to Keats as he lay in bed in an upstairs room at the Hunt house where he'd been transferred by his friend the day after the attack. Kindly Mrs. Hunt and several servants were now caring for him, preparing dishes he could eat easily and trying to keep down the noise created by five rambunctious children. Already he'd been examined several times by the two doctors, who had rendered their verdicts about Italy in early July. Relaying the news about the decision to his sister, he adds something else the physicians said: "I have no hopes of an entire reestablishment of my

Health under some months of patience . . . which I am now practicing better than I ever thought it possible for me." A full recovery this time would not be rapid.

Since the hemorrhage on the twenty-second he'd brought up no more blood, and with each day he felt he was "getting a little stronger." But he'd been given a scare, and had been hit hard physically, a fact mirrored all too obviously in his ravaged countenance. His appearance, reported one visiter, in particular the face, was "shocking and now reminds me of poor Tom," while another caller about the same time wrote that Keats "never spoke and looks emaciated." However, starting in mid-July, about three weeks after the attack, he began to bounce back and was soon well enough to leave the house twice a day for half-hour walks up and down busy Mortimer Terrace. Along with fresh air and mild exercise, these walks helped pull him out of his lethargy, for the street as he pictured it was "very much pester'd with cries, ballad singers, and street music."

Whether Fanny's reply to Keats' two anguished letters of mid-June reached him before the attack on the twenty-second or afterward in his sick room at Hunt's cannot be said. Nor is it known whether she visited him at Hunt's (she did send flowers, which he kept in a vase on the table by his bed, and on his finger was a ring she'd given him.) In any case, his acknowledgement of her letter, with answering comment of his own, was not written until he'd experienced some return of strength, probably in the second week of July when his outings along Mortimer Terrace began. The letter is a rambling effort but quite revealing, its burden being his undying love for her coupled with an apology and a strenuous denial that he'd ever so much as thought of separation.

"My head is puzzled this morning, and I scarce know what I shall say though I am full of a hundred things," he begins in fairly relaxed fashion. But then he promptly stumbles into another stabbing remark, saying he would "rather be writing to you this morning, notwithstanding the alloy of grief in such an occupation, than enjoy any other pleasure, with health to boot, unconnected with you." He gets off an apology, curiously half-hearted, for his two letters, explaining lamely that "those words have been wrung from me by the sharpness of my feelings." He would be more contrite, more openly penitent, he adds pointedly, would reject all suspicions, "could I believe that I did it without any cause" —words that prove beyond doubt that he'd heard *something*.

On the question of breaking their engagement, he asks plaintively, "Do you suppose it possible I could ever leave you?" What he wrote in those previous letters that seemed threatening had been torn from him by "the spirit of Wretchedness in myself," and were never meant to imply a warning or threat of separation. "My fairest, my delicious, my angel Fanny! do not believe me such a vulgar fellow."

As for those few among his friends who dared to laugh at her— yes! there were some, he admitted, "and I never shall think of them again as friends or even acquaintances . . . If I am the Theme, I will not be the friend of idle gossips." Pay no attention to "those Laughers," he urges, for they were only jealous of her, envying her wit, her charm, her Beauty. If they could, they would long ago have "God-bless'd-me from you forever . . . plying me with disencouragements with respect to you eternally." He ends by repeating his one constant hope or wish in regard to their love, still in some frustration so far as he could tell: "Let me be but certain that you are mine heart and soul, and I could die more happily than I could otherwise live."

His vowing to cut himself off from "those Laughers" was at least partly an empty pose, and they both knew it. The offenders included some who, while not laughing, did seriously question the match, and who could never be ignored, not only Charles Brown and the Dilkes, but Fanny's own mother. Brown quite honestly felt that Fanny had "many faults," and as Fanny herself later conceded, he simply didn't much like the girl, in particular questioning whether she was quite serious in her feelings for his friend.

The Dilkes' view was contained in a single short paragraph in one of Mrs. Dilke's letters, which also reveals how Mrs. Brawne regarded the situation. "It is quite a settled thing," wrote Mrs. Dilke, "between John Keats and Miss Brawne—God help them. The mother says she can't prevent it, and that her only hope is that it will go off." Another sentence in that passage, short as it is, throws an additional sharp light on the objections these Laughers had to the match—they spotted a trait in the poet which would give concern to anyone with sense: "He don't like anyone to look at or speak to her." As even her friends admitted, Fanny could rightly be censured for her cute and overly familiar ways with young men. But Keats' reaction to it all was too possessive, his jealousy downright unhealthy, frenzied at times. Never mind the obvious question as to whether the two were well suited otherwise, *here* was a dangerously corrosive basis for any marriage.

(The Dilke estimate of Fanny spread through the whole family and descended through the generations. In 1875, Dilke's grandson received a letter from his great-uncle William, in part of which he discusses Fanny's character. "My recollection of Miss Brawne as a girl agrees with your grandmother's description. She was of a very sallow complexion, not a lady with whom a poet so sensitive as John Keats would be likely to fall in love. Your grandfather would probably say she made the advances to him without really caring much for him.")

Keats' best and most understanding friend, John Reynolds, also saw the engagement as a mistake, and didn't hesitate to let his opinion be known. Hearing that Keats was off to Italy for his health, he said in a letter that he was very glad, since among other things, "Absence from the poor idle Thing of womankind, to whom he has so unaccountably attached himself, will not be an ill thing." With this view, Reynolds' three sisters were in full agreement, one of them referring in a note of July to "a connexion which has been a most unhappy one for him." (The charge that the Reynolds family were all down on Fanny because Keats had failed to pick a wife from among the three Reynolds girls would hold up better if so many others had not spoken out. All these people, it should be noted, knew each other well. Mrs. Dilke was not only close to Mrs. Brawne, she was a "great friend" of Fanny herself, then and for long afterward.)

Fanny's obscurer relatives—she had four married aunts, sisters of her mother, all of whom had children—had opinions about her too. One of them, a cousin, many years later went on record when he

joined the debate that erupted with publication of the Keats love letters. The accuracy of the report in some respects may be questioned
by anyone so inclined, but its existence may not be ignored:

> Miss Fanny Brawne was very fond of admiration. I do not think
> she cared for Keats, although she was engaged to him. She was very
> much affected when he died, because she had treated him so badly.
> She was very fond of dancing, and of going to the opera and to
> balls and parties . . . Through the Dilkes, Miss Brawne was invited
> out a great deal, and as Keats was not in robust health to take her
> out himself (for he never went with her) she used to go with mili-
> tary men to the Woolwich balls and to balls in Hampstead; and she
> used to dance with these officers a great deal more than Keats
> liked . . .
>
> Although she was not a great beauty she was very lively and
> agreeable. I remember that among those frequenting Mrs.
> Brawne's house in Hampstead were a number of foreign gentle-
> men. Keats thought that she talked and flirted and danced too
> much with them, but his remonstrances were all unheeded . . .

Even Keats' brother George, back in England on a quick business
trip in 1820, became a witness in the matter, a witness at least to the
fact that derogatory talk about Fanny was then in circulation. Arriving in January, just prior to Keats' first hemorrhage, he soon heard,
and believed, some stories about Fanny from unnamed sources
("persons I very much respect"). What the stories were he never told,
saying only that they painted her as "an artful bad hearted Girl."
Carefully he adds that when in her company he never noticed anything to support the charge, except a degree of petulance.

Fanny's own statements, made to Keats' sister, are also to be considered, here only briefly. "All that grieves me now," she wrote shortly
after his death, "is that I was not with him, and so near it as I was . . .
had he returned I should have been his wife and he would have lived
with us." Two months after that she again touched on the topic,
insisting that of all who had known him, *she* had "loved him best,"

adding that her loss was irreparable. "To no one but you would I mention him. I will suffer no one but you to speak to me of him . . . I have not got over it and never shall."

Whether those words, and others similar, can bear the weight put on them by Fanny's adherents is a question to be faced further along. Here, in necessary anticipation, it must be admitted that, despite vowing she wouldn't, she did indeed eventually get over her loss. Several years afterward, while Keats' name was still in eclipse, she wondered how she had ever been attracted to so unpromising a young man, and said so in plain words. But that is the least of the peculiarities to be met in the later life of Fanny Brawne.

Early in August, depressed by the thought that in a matter of weeks he would be leaving England to face an uncertain future in a foreign land, Keats wrote what turned out to be his final letter to Fanny. It gives pathetic witness to the misery he felt as he went on his last journey, still in doubt, still wary as to the true feelings of the girl he loved.

Over and over he complains that he will never survive the separation from her, that in her he is "concentrated," and apart from her sees "no prospect of any rest." He declares himself "sickened at the brute world which you are smiling with." For him the future forebodes "nothing but thorns." Then in a fleetingly graphic, one-sentence sketch he tells why: "Suppose me in Rome—well, I should there see you as in a magic glass going to and from town at all hours."

In his woe he gropes for a slight act of reassurance on Fanny's part, actually asking her to rewrite part of a letter she'd sent him recently. "I enclose a passage from one of your letters which I want you to alter a little—I want (if you will have it so) the matter expressed less coldly to me." It is not known that Fanny complied with so curious a request, though very probably she did, and it stands as a most revealing incident. What Fanny wrote initially in the letter doesn't concern him, that distant tone, or note or remark, and what it might imply as to their relationship. He only wants the offending passage made right, softened, muted so that in his lonely lodging in Rome he may read and reread the letter untroubled.

Leaping from Keats' last letter comes still another arresting sentence, again curiously revealing, and no surprise in its calling on Shakespeare to bear him witness. "Shakespeare always sums up matters in the most sovereign manner," he writes abruptly. "Hamlet's heart was full of such Misery as mine is when he said to Ophelia, 'Go to a Nunnery, go, go!' " That is the full extent of the mention but it leads to one more unflattering comment on Fanny.

In Hamlet's famous scene with Ophelia, immediately following the "To be or not to be" soliloquy, the brooding Prince four times refers to nunneries, of course symbolically, in different words (none phrased exactly as Keats has it). But Hamlet's grief comes not from jealousy or from any personal wariness over the conduct of a woman, so what was Keats thinking when he said that Hamlet's misery was the same as his? What Keats had in mind in making his remark, surely, were the words in which Hamlet paints what he sees as the falseness and fickleness of women, their ability to deceive and manipulate men.

"Get thee to a nunnery," orders Hamlet, " . . . Or if thou wilt needs marry, marry a fool; for wise men know well enough what monsters you make of them." With wonderful economy he then lists his notion of the ways in which women exert their purposeful charm, all precisely fitting Fanny. "God hath given you one face, and you make yourselves another. You jig, you amble, and you lisp. You nickname God's creatures and make your wantonness your ignorance. Go to, I'll no more on't! It hath made me mad."

Not always did Keats think of Cressida when silently stewing over one or another of Fanny's unescorted outings. Hamlet's words, too, must often have run through his mind.

"If my health would bear it," Keats goes on in his letter, "I could write a Poem which I have in my head, which would be a consolation for people in such a situation as mine. I would show someone in Love as I am, with a person living in such Liberty as you do." The poem was actually written, his last. It is a short poem of seven stanzas, each stanza having eight lines, all quite uninspired, which yet manage to preserve the rawness in one young poet's confused heart. Two of the seven will suffice, both making clear the largely sexual basis of his concern:

> Who now with greedy looks eats up my feast?
>   What stare outfaces now my silver moon!
> Ah! keep that hand unravished at the least;
>   Let, let the amorous burn—
>   But prythee, do not turn
> The current of your heart from me so soon.
>   O! save, in charity,
>   The quickest pulse for me.

> Ah! if you prize my subdued soul above
>   The poor, the fading, brief, pride of an hour;
> Let none profane my Holy See of love,
>   Or with a rude hand break
>   The sacramental cake:
> Let none else touch the just new-budded flower;
>   If not—may my eyes close,
>   Love! on their last repose.

On August 12th, with his departure for Italy only a month off, he made a last desperate move to gain some temporary peace of mind, perhaps also to gather some few more pleasant moments for remembering in his exile. Deliberately he picked a fight with his amazed host—a letter, from Fanny it is said, was accidentally opened before it was delivered to his room—and he stormed out of the Hunt residence. Straight to Wentworth Place he headed, supposedly for a quick stop on his way to new lodgings, but all too transparently with a grim determination to be taken in.

He got his wish. The motherly Mrs. Brawne, appalled by the haggard, pleading look that greeted her on the doorstep, would not allow him to go off to distant, barren lodgings by himself. For his final weeks in England, Keats stayed with the Brawne family in

Hampstead, the mother, the two girls, and the brother. More or less contentedly, he lived under the very same roof, sat daily at the same table, as Fanny.

During that time some earnest talk would have occupied the two, but only one of their topics is known: whether Fanny and her mother should accompany the poet to Italy. Nothing urgent, just then, bound them to England, and all recognized that the tender nursing of familiar hands, even aside from the tonic of Fanny's presence, would make a profound difference in the well-being of the sick man. All that can be known, however, of that crucial conversation is the little that Fanny wrote later, recording the fact that it was Keats' own decision that the women not go. As she explained, that decision "was a good deal through his kindness for me for he foresaw what would happen." What he feared *might* happen would be closer to the reality, his fear of growing much worse, from whatever cause, becoming bedridden and perhaps dying, an ordeal he wished to spare his young love.

It was a brave decision for Keats to have made. At that time the name of Joseph Severn as a possible companion had not yet come up and he knew that he was facing the prospect of many months of dreary solitude, worse if he should further sicken. On that score, interestingly, he remained hopeful, at least regarding the most dire of the various possibilities. Writing his sister in mid-August, he says his illness "was not yet Consumption, I believe, but it would be were I to remain in this climate all Winter."

When at last he departed to board his ship at a dock just outside London, a few days prior to sailing, in his bag were several small gifts from the Brawnes. Included was one unusual little item Fanny had given him in response to his earnest request that she "invent some means to make me at all happy without you." It was an oval carnelian, about the size and shape of an egg, a smooth stone of reddish-white chalcedony just right for caressing in the palm of the hand.

FOUR

GOOD SPIRITS AND
HOPEFUL FELLOWS

From the large front windows of his house in the Piazza di Spagna, Dr. James Clark had an unobstructed view of the broad Spanish Steps, directly opposite, mounting grandly up the steep hill to the twin-towered church at the summit.

Also in view, fronting the piazza at the right of the Steps, was the house at No. 26. Here some time earlier Dr. Clark had personally arranged for the rental of a small flat to be used by his newest patient, John Keats, due to arrive any day. But to the waiting Clark, Mr. Keats was not just another of the many ailing English residents he attended in Rome. Of a literary turn, familiar with all three of Keats' volumes, he was among those who expected marvelous things to flow from the pen of the young poet as he matured. Just recently he'd read, and been much pleased by, a very good notice in the *Edinburgh Review* of Keats' latest volume, published only months before. "I feel very much interested in him," wrote Clark to a friend in England, "and believe me will do everything in my power to be of service."

In fact, Clark's presence in the city was the primary reason why Keats and his physicians chose Rome as a haven from the ravages of winter. A native of Scotland, trained in the leading medical schools at Edinburgh, at age thirty-two Clark was already a prominent authority on a comparatively new branch of medicine, the beneficial effects of temperate climates in treating chronic illness. His book on the subject, a pioneer work, had been published in Edinburgh earlier that same year. Its title, aiming at completeness, occupied an entire page, a display felt to be needed because of the subject's newness, even among doctors: *Medical Notes on Climate, Diseases, Hospitals, and Medical Schools in France, Italy, Switzerland; Comprising an Inquiry into the Effects of a Residence in the South of Europe in Cases of Pulmonary Consumption, and Illustrating the Present State of Medicine in Those Countries.* The title of a second, revised edition ran even longer but was generally known as *The Influence of Climate In the Prevention and Cure of Chronic Diseases.*

In the book many possible sites in southern Europe were discussed but Rome was preferred, with Nice and Naples close behind. "The great numbers of our countrymen who annually resort to this wonderful city," said Clark in an introduction, "and the circumstances of its not unfrequently being preferred as a winter residence by the invalid will, I hope, render the following observations on its climate, imperfect as they are, acceptable to the medical reader."

Rome's climate, he explained, was warmer and moister, conditions much to be preferred, and was also a great deal freer from those "dry, cold winds" so keenly felt elsewhere. Almost every day of the year in Rome, when it didn't rain, an invalid might enjoy "a couple of hours exercise on the Pincian mount . . . without being exposed to the direct influence of the sun's rays." Over and over, he added, Rome's wonderful benefits for the sufferer had been demonstrated to him by actual cases. One man, "labouring under an affection of the lungs," left Rome for Naples where he soon afterward began to spit blood and was "obliged to return to Rome, where he always feels comfortable." The same experience had occurred to another of his patients, a man much troubled by cough and chest pain. Naples had greatly aggravated the condition, yet when the man returned to Rome, "these unpleasant symptoms very soon disappeared." Within the city itself, Clark advised, "the best residence is somewhere about the Piazza di Spagna, which is well sheltered, and has the advantage of being close to the Pincian Mount, which affords the best protected and most delightful walks at Rome."

But there was a caution. For the invalid, Rome could also be a dangerous place, tempting him to neglect sensible behavior. The recovering invalid "must not imagine that he can enter with impunity into those amusements from which he was prohibited at home." Many of the typical houses of Rome, for instance, "were not well calculated for gaiety during winter . . . the staircases and lobbies are large and open, and subject to currents of air, of which invalids not unfrequently feel the effects." Very often, also, the streets in the central city were "damp and chilly, and the alternation between these shaded streets and situations exposed to the sun is often very great." The open carriages so much liked by the Romans could also be a hazard, "very dangerous to the delicate," when passing from shade into sunlight. Closed carriages were much to be preferred as keeping the temnperature even.

Most importantly, the ancient city's main attractions, its many famous ruins and even most of the big contemporary churches, must at all costs be avoided by the invalid. Such places were "frequently damp and always cold . . . ladies in particular visiting these churches should be careful to protect themselves by warm thick shoes from the extreme coldness of the marble floors."

By mid-November, Keats had not shown up, though he'd written from Naples announcing his arrival in Italy. On the fifteenth, somewhat concerned, Clark sat down to write a colleague in the other city asking him to make some inquiries. While he was writing, a servant brought word that two young Englishmen were at the door, a Mr. Keats and a Mr. Severn. Happily greeting the two, Clark learned that the journey up from Naples had taken longer than usual—no less than eight days, the travelers favoring a leisurely pace. They had also taken a less frequented route, proceeding by way of Pozzuoli, Terracina, and Velletri. Their hired *vettura*, a small, upright, enclosed carriage, had crawled along covering hardly twenty-five miles a day.

The pace had been so relaxed, and the countryside so inviting, that Severn had often climbed down to walk beside the moving vehicle, allowing Keats room to stretch out. The only real disappointment had been the different wayside inns where they'd halted each night. Accommodations at these, as Severn recalled, were "villainously coarse and unpalatable" (perhaps only the usual reaction of neophyte travelers unwilling to try new things). That morning they had entered Rome by the Lateran Gate and had promptly come upon the Colosseum, "superb in its stupendous size and rugged grandeur." But to the anxious travelers, intent less on scenery than on reaching medical care, the most welcome sight in all of Rome was the "genial face" of Dr. Clark.

Shown the apartment at No. 26, the two were well pleased and began settling in. Their landlady was a middle-aged woman named Anna Angeletti—described as "lively, smart, handsome" —who with her two young daughters occupied space at the building's rear on both second and third floors (Mr. Angeletti seemed always to be away from home on business). The other apartments in the house were also occupied: a retired Englishman on the floor below, a young Irishman and an Italian army officer in separate flats above, all of them attended by live-in servants. In the whole building Keats and Severn were the only residents shifting for themselves, getting only occasional help with household chores from the landlady's servant girl.

While not spacious, the flat was comfortably and even elegantly furnished, meant to accommodate a small family or two friends. Soon an additional piece was added, a small piano rented from the landlady. Severn who was quite an accomplished pianist (taught by his father, a music master), reasoned that Keats, who was "passionately fond of music," would be calmed and soothed by daily sessions of his playing lasting perhaps an hour or so. Dr. Clark, readily agreeing, loaned the two a huge pile of sheet music.

The tiny room overlooking the Spanish Steps just off Keats' bedroom was hardly bigger than a walk-in closet but had its own large window. This Severn took for himself, setting up his easel and arranging his painting things. Already in mind as his subject he had an ambitious idea: the death of Alcibiades, the Athenian statesman assassinated by the Spartans. It was to be a large picture including at least eight figures and much elaborate drapery. Within a few days of moving in, urged by Keats to lose no time, he was at work trying preliminary sketches.

Like most foreigners then living in furnished rooms in Rome, the newcomers at No. 26 duly arranged to have their evening meal sent in to them on a regular basis from a local *trattoria*. At agreed times each day a porter would appear at the door carrying a large tin-lined basket, its cover shut tight to keep the food hot. This service was also supplied by their landlady whose *trattoria* was located in the building next door. In this case, however, the usual arrangement quickly produced an odd bit of behavior on the part of the poet, not quite characteristic and apparently arising from the unthinking bravado of youth. An incident always told with an indulgent smile by biographers, in reality the episode earned the two men the settled ill will of the landlady, who it seems happened to be present, later causing them considerable difficulty.

After several evenings of being served "bad dinners," each day more uninviting despite "cunning disguises in sauces and spices," and complaining to no effect, Keats vowed to take direct action. On the sixth or seventh evening as the porter set his basket on the table and began laying out the steaming dishes—macaroni, a fowl, cauliflower, and rice pudding, says Severn—Keats stood calmly watching. Then without a word he picked up each dish in turn, walked to the open window overlooking the building's entrance, extended his arm, turned his hand over, and emptied the contents of the dish unto the pavement two stories below. His little performance ended, he then "quietly but very decidedly pointed to the basket for the porter to take away, which he did without demur." Shortly afterward, the porter returned with another dinner steaming in his basket, this time "an excellent one," and no longer was food a problem.

Telling the story years later, Severn thought he remembered how it had all been done "to the amusement of the porter and the *padrona di casa*," the landlady, who had the grace not to charge for the discarded meal. Implied is a sort of grudging admiration on the part of landlady and porter for so spirited an action, a view of the incident accepted ever since. But as will be seen, Signora Angeletti, who may or may not have been present but who in any case would have had to arrange for the cleaning up of the mess at her front door, actually had been far from amused.

Before doing his full examination of the poet, Dr. Clark allowed him a few days to rest up from his bumpy carriage ride over the unpaved Italian roads. Then, cautiously, he preferred to hold off on his conclusions until he'd made a second examination, so it was near the end of November when he finally informed the nervous Keats of his findings. Happily, they accorded precisely with the opinions reached earlier by the doctors in London.

The ailment was not consumption. Chiefly, while it eluded exact diagnosis, the trouble appeared to be "seated in his Stomach," though there was also "some suspicion" about the heart. Concerning the lungs, he didn't feel at all sure. They might be involved, but if so, to a much less extent. The poet's "mental exertions and application I think have been the sources of his complaints," Clark wrote a friend, echoing almost precisely the London physicians, whose opinions he'd probably been told. "If I can put his mind at ease I think he'll do well."

Until he could learn more, said Clark, he would prescribe the usual regimen of rest, regular daily outings for a walk, and proper diet. He also ordered a daily session of horseback riding, an hour or so over the pleasant courses of the Pincian Hill, or along the Tiber. Arrangements for a mount could be made at any of the numerous livery stables in the vicinity. That part of the prescription, so strange to modern eyes, would not in the least have surprised Keats or Severn. Horseback riding for certain classes of chronic invalids, including consumptives in the early stages, by then had long been standard treatment, founded on the best medical opinion.

The movement of a trotting or even galloping horse, it was felt, exercised the rider's body without requiring of him any physical exertion aside from a tension in arms and legs, or putting him out of breath. It also provided fresh air and a frequent change of scene, so necessary to an optimistic mental outlook. Unguessed, of course, was the fact that for a tuberculous patient, and others as well, rest was far more important than any sort of exercise. Use of a horse was promptly arranged, and from almost the first day Keats went out for a morning ride, never moving at more than a canter.

Of some special if collateral interest is the question of *how* Dr. Clark went about making his examination of the sick man. Only the year before in Paris, Clark had encountered one of medicine's great breakthroughs, a newly invented instrument which for the first time allowed a doctor to probe the interior of the human thorax by interpreting sound. This was the stethoscope, then a long, thin tube of wood, recently perfected by Rene Laennec. Much aroused by the stethoscope's potential in diagnosis, its ability to provide, as he said, "much useful information in distinguishing diseases," Clark had observed its use by Laennec at the Necker Hospital in Paris. Back in England he tried it himself for a time in his practice, but disappointingly as he admits in his book, he was in too much of a hurry: it would, he decided, "require more time than I had to bestow to make myself fully acquainted with the use of this instrument." By the fall of 1820, however, more than a year later, faced in the ailing Keats with a case that cried out for the application of the stethoscope, he well may have tried to use it, his knowledge of the technique perhaps proving still inadequate. If he did did not employ it at this first examination of Keats in November, it does appear certain that he used it later, and properly, when he at last gave a verdict confirming the presence of consumption.

Clark's final bit of diagnosis was not a medical one, but personal, and concerned not Keats but Severn himself. The sick man's companion, it seems, had not impressed the physician any more than he had his own acquaintances in London. "He has a friend with him who seems very attentive to him," wrote Clark, "but between you & I is not the best suited for his companion, but I suppose poor fellow he had no choice." Severn's affable manner and smiling disposition—true, a degree of naivete—it appears was seen by many as an inadequate prop for genius.

Three days after receiving Clark's hopeful diagnosis, Keats wrote a short letter to Charles Brown (the last of his letters to survive and probably the last written). Though he was at this time physically comfortable, unbothered by cough or bodily weakness, emotionally he was suffering, a fact made plain in the letter's opening sentences. Barely does he manage to skirt the real reason for his depression, his whirling thoughts of Fanny:

My Dear Brown,
    'Tis the most difficult thing in the world for me to write a letter. My stomach continues so bad that I feel it worse on opening any book—yet I am much better than I was in Quarantine. Then I was afraid to encounter the proing and conning of anything interesting to me in England. I have an habitual feeling of my real life having past, and that I am leading a posthumous existence. God knows how it would have been—but it appears to me—however, I will not speak of that subject . . .

Besides worry over Fanny, and perhaps some growing regret that he'd stopped her from coming with him to Italy, he now feels more and more miserable over another absence in his life, that of the writing of poetry, an activity still forbidden him. "There is one thought enough to kill me," he writes. "I have been well, healthy, alert, etc., walking with her—and now—the knowledge of contrast, feeling for light and shade, all that information (primitive sense) necessary for a poem are great enemies to the recovery of the stomach." Fanny and poetry, the two things he found most essential to his well-being, were both gone from him, the one a thousand miles away, the other, as it seemed in his dejection, even farther.

Within a day or two after Clark's examination the daily routine had begun. Usually Keats slept well, so his nights were passed in some refreshing comfort. Each morning Severn would awaken first, about eight, would quietly rise from his couch-bed in the larger room, careful to make no noise that might disturb Keats in his smaller chamber. Dressing, he'd leave the apartment for a walk round the broad Piazza, stopping at the fountain to enjoy the sound of the plashing water. Returning, he would bring with him a container of fresh milk for breakfast, purchased from one of the farmers who early each morning drove cows into the piazza where servants and housewives waited. By nine o'clock Keats would be up and the two would sit down to breakfast, prepared by Severn in the fireplace, sometimes brought in by the landlady's girl. Breakfast done, Keats would go out for his ride.

Many afternoons there were outings along the elegant Via del Corso, into busy, spacious Piazza del Popolo or, in the opposite direction, the Piazza Venetia. There were hours of strolling on the Pincian Hill amid the profusion of olive and ilex trees, so well laid out, or lounging at the boat-fountain in the piazza a few feet from his own door. In calm serenity the days went pleasantly by, and more and more the poet settled into an acceptance of his two losses, even if grudgingly. Both, as he was now increasingly convinced, had escaped him only temporarily.

On his own, Severn went off to visit the Colosseum and the other ancient monuments, as well as many churches and picture galleries, all forbidden to Keats by Clark's edict. The Colosseum, in particular, vividly impressed the inexperienced Severn, a result he eagerly relayed to an appreciative Keats each time he returned from an excursion:

> How well I remember risking my life in getting a wall flower on a ledge of the Colosseum, for Keats to feel how all the air could be scented by its perfume! The eye was doubly charmed with the grandeur of antiquity in its noblest forms, and with the sweet freshness of nature exulting over all its lofty walls and precipitous ledges. The huge ruins, consisting of massive boulders, amazed me, for I wondered how the latter were ever lifted and joined . . . In this way I saw many of the finest ruins at the most favourable moment, and was able to entertain Keats with my descriptions . . .

Through Clark, Severn was also introduced to another young English artist in the city, the then well-known sculptor, John Gibson, who welcomed Severn to his studio only a few blocks from No. 26. The day Severn first showed up at Gibson's place an important visitor had just arrived there, the English art collector, Lord Colchester. Diffidently, Severn was bowing himself out of the way when Gibson took his arm and brought him back, throughout the visit showing him equal attention with the noble lord. Much struck by this graceful act "toward a poor and unknown young artist like myself," Severn joyfully decided that Rome "is the place for me!" Told the story that evening, a delighted Keats echoed the sentiment.

Severn also had with him a letter of introduction to another, more celebrated artist then living and working in Rome, the sculptor Antonio Canova. Severn did call on him and was well received but left scant record of what transpired (they "had a pipe and a pot together ... He has promised me his services at any time ... he seems to think highly of my views"). Canova soon came up in another connection, however, offering the two friends their only brush with the Italian *haute monde*.

At a palatial residence not far from the Piazza di Spagna lived the Princess Pauline, estranged wife of one of the world's richest men, Prince Camillo Borghese, and sister of Napoleon (then in exile on St. Helena). A celebrated if aging beauty, Pauline was then entering her forties and was widely known in the city's social circles for her amorous adventuring. When Keats and Severn arrived, the many scandalous stories circulating about her included a nude statue of herself recently completed by Canova at her commission. It was, they soon learned, then on display at the Villa Borghese where the public were flocking to see it. While nude statues were nothing new in Rome, no living woman would ever confess to having posed for one, something that this princess did defiantly.

As did everyone else, Keats and Severn went to see the statue, and found it only half nude (drapery covered the hips, while the torso, bare from the stomach up, half reclined on pillows. The left hand held a symbolic apple.). Wonderfully executed, it was still, thought Severn along with most viewers, "in beautiful bad taste." Agreeing, Keats quipped that its most fitting name would be *The Aeolian Harp*, that instrument played on by every stray wind, as rumor claimed the lady was.

That would have been the end of the story except that soon afterward, the two began to encounter the princess herself in their strolls along the promenades and bridal paths of the Pincio. By then they had made the acquaintance of another Englishman who often joined in their walks, an army officer named Lieutenant Isaac Elton. Also an invalid, but a tall, handsome, distinguished figure in his uniform, Elton was soon spotted by the princess when walking with her retinue or riding in an open carriage. Thereafter, said Severn, in passing Keats and his companions she would "cast languishing glances upon Lieutenant Elton each time we encountered her. At last this so jarred upon Keats' nerves, though he thankfully acknowledged that he was not the attraction, that we were obliged to go and take our walk in another place. Elton gladly enough acquiesced."

Why Keats should have been so resentful of the lady's interest in the lieutenant, why he didn't take the aging coquette to be the sadly amusing spectacle she was, isn't explained by Severn. If he didn't know, however, he might have guessed. In the person of the shamelessly flirting princess, Keats found an all too penetrating reminder of the girl he'd left behind him in Hampstead. "As in a magic glass" — the scene he'd drawn in his last letter—he saw Fanny as she went "to and from town at all hours," admitting in another letter, written in Naples, that "my imagination is horribly vivid about her—I see her—I hear her." Nor would it be surprising if his overworked imagination carried him to the ugly extreme of picturing Fanny as she would be ten or twenty years hence, still engaged like the pathetic princess in seeking the passing attention of men. Little wonder that he insisted the trio take its walks anywhere but on the Pincian Hill.

In addition to Lieutenant Elton, a few further acquaintances were made, particularly among the city's large and quite active English art colony. Only one or two names are known definitely, however, those of Richard Westmacott, an architect, and William Ewing, a young sculptor. With Ewing, Keats and Severn enjoyed their chief friendship in Rome, aside from Dr. Clark, the sculptor coming often to visit at No. 26.

Whatever the cause, life in Rome did indeed have a beneficial effect on Keats. Three weeks after taking possession of the flat he even seemed physically stronger. His "bright falcon eyes," as Severn called them, were clear and steady, giving promise of continued improvement, a hope that was much encouraged by Dr. Clark's own bouyant attitude. Aside from his never-ceasing agitation over Fanny, mentally and emotionally Keats had also been able to achieve some balance. He had even begun on poetry again, not yet actually writing but seriously planning another long narrative.

The topic this time was Sabrina, the river-goddess pictured in Milton's *Comus*. On the details of this classic tale, recalled Severn, Keats would dwell with "immense enthusiasm," reciting Milton's lines aloud "in a manner I will remember to the end of my days." The new poem would illustrate "some points of English history and character," a departure for Keats, its animating principal to be "moral Beauty." But here again Fanny Brawne intrudes, for in fact she is readily identified as the poem's main inspirer. The whole duty of the goddess Sabrina (known in legend even before Milton) was to aid distressed maidens, specifically those who faced a threat to their virginity. In writing the poem, Keats would in a sense be invoking Sabrina's watchful care on behalf of the footloose young woman he'd left so far behind.

In the licentious lines Milton gives to *Comus*, Keats would have found a graphic and disturbing presentation of the young lady he knew so well:

> List, Lady; be not coy and be not cozened
> With that same vaunted name, Virginity.
> Beauty is Nature's coin; must not be hoarded,
> But must be current; and the good thereof
> Consists in mutual and partaken bliss,
> Unsavory in the enjoyment of itself.

If you let slip time, like a neglected rose
It withers on the stalk with languished head.
Beauty is Nature's brag, and must be shown
In courts, at feasts, and high solemnities,
where most may wonder at the workmanship . . .

Keats' interest in writing about Sabrina surely came from Milton's depiction of the goddess as able to preserve and guard unwary young ladies who are too often seen unescorted at courts, feasts, and high solemnities—not to mention dinner parties, card parties, the theater, dances, and military balls:

. . . as the old swain said, she can unlock
The clasping charm, and thaw the numbing spell,
If she be right invoked in warbled song;
For maidenhood she loves, and will be swift
To aid a virgin, such as was herself,
In hard besetting need . . .

In England, all the waiting friends had by now gotten word of Keats' safe arrival in Italy. The letters sent from Naples by both men the day after landing had taken just over three weeks to reach London, a transmittal time for mail that would hold true for all their subsequent exchanges both ways. Gratefully received was Severn's assurance in the letter to Haslam that in spite of all difficulties, "We are in good spirits and I may say hopeful fellows." It was a comment immensely welcome at Wentworth Place, and at a dozen other households.

Severn's letter itself Haslam had sent round the circle, eventually reaching Brown who took it over to the Brawnes in the other half of the house. "Thank you for the enclosed," he wrote Haslam when returning the letter. "I read it next door, skipping and adding, without the slightest suspicion on their part." Pointedly, he adds that Keats' letter to him of November 1st, with its heavy lament over his being so cruelly separated from Fanny, he has *not* shown to the

Brawnes. "I wish I might—the showing of it would even relieve me, for the thought of it quite weighs me down."

Close in spirit to the poet as Brown was, knowing as well, and seeing every day, the young lady who was the cause of his friend's pain, it is no surprise that Keats' anguished letter weighed him down. Many times he must have read, and reread it, pausing over some of the starker phrases, wondering whether any change had occurred in the three weeks since the words were penned:

O, God! God! God! Everything I have in my trunks that reminds me of her goes through me like a spear . . . O that I could be buried near where she lives! . . . Where can I look for consolation or ease? If I had any chance of recovery, this passion would kill me . . . Oh, Brown, I have coals of fire in my breast . . .

FIVE

THIS POSTHUMOUS LIFE

Not once had Joseph Severn stopped to think what his life might be like if his delicate companion should sicken further while they were alone in Italy. As he later admitted, in his eager rush to join the poet whom he looked on as inexorably headed for greatness, he had no fears, no hesitations, but "only thought of the beautiful mind of Keats, my attachment to him, and his convalescence."

That there existed some real chance of a setback, of renewed serious illness, perhaps worse than any of the earlier attacks, Severn knew very well. But with the willing blindness of youth he had refused to dwell on so dire a possibility, or to think how it might alter his own circumstances. Begining on the morning of December 9th, all too suddenly and shockingly, he found out. The most harrowing months of Severn's young life, never to be forgotten, were at hand.

Rising early on the ninth, he went for his usual walk in the piazza, posted several letters home, then on the way back stopped to buy the milk for breakfast. Entering the apartment, he found Keats already up and dressed, and in "unusual good spirits." As the two prepared breakfast, Keats continued talking in a light vein and smiling easily, in fact was "going on merrily."

Then Severn heard Keats cough, hard and raspingly, then again,

harder, then a third time, and abruptly he was seized by a fit of continued violent coughing that bent him double. Dragging a handker-
chief out of his pocket, he raised it to his mouth as the blood came
spilling from his lips.

At first, Severn stood and watched, feeling helpless. Then as he saw
Keats' shoulders heaving he realized that the cough, unable to loosen
the phlegm, had turned to retching. He rushed to support his stag-
gering friend, and was appalled to see the blood spurt from his
mouth. Reaching for something to catch the flow, he held it in place,
and when the fit had subsided and Keats, exhausted and sweating
profusely, had thrown himself on the couch. The spattered bowl in
Severn's hand held "near two Cup-fuls of blood."

Instantly, leaving Keats stretched limply on the couch, Severn
dashed out the door and down the stairs, raced across the piazza to
the Clark home, where he found the doctor up and ready for the
day's work. Bag in hand, Clark ran back across the piazza beside the
excited Severn. They found Keats still on the couch and feverish, and
Clark immediately bared the poet's arm and proceeded to draw off
more blood. He took a full eight ounces, says Severn, "black and thick
in the extreme" (of course, unknowingly inducing further weakness
in the sufferer). The two then led him back to his own room where
they helped him undress and climb into bed.

When Clark finally left he instructed Severn to call him at any
time if needed, and he would be back that evening for another look.
Keats was to remain in bed, and he was to be given no solid food, at
most some milk if wanted. The intake of food must be drastically
reduced in order to depress the flow of blood (the deprivation of
food also lessening the patient's vitality).

The apartment was now calm, but Severn's ordeal that day was
just beginning. "O what an awful day!" he would sigh in welcome
relief after the tumult had finally lessened.

After Keats had lain quietly for some time, while Severn was in the
other room he roused up suddenly, threw back the covers, and
rushed wide-eyed from his bedroom. He would kill himself, he
shouted wildly, he wouldn't submit to a lingering death as had his

brother: "This day shall be my last!" Severn, after quoting those words adds feelingly, "but for me most certainly it would."

Rummaging frantically in closets and desk drawers, Keats searched for the little box of medicines the two always kept on hand. In it, he knew, was a bottle of laudanum bought at a chemist's shop before they left England (a product then freely available). One good swallow of that pernicious liquid would end it all—an overdose of laudanum, in fact, was the nineteenth century's commonest means of suicide. Reaching the bottle first, Severn ignored his friend's pleading that he give it up. Then he went round the apartment gathering all the knives, scissors, glass objects, and sharp-bladed instruments he could find, "took every destroying means from his reach, nor let him be from my sight one minute."

The long hours wore on, Severn hovering near his friend as he lay on a sofa or moaning on his bed. Dr. Clark's visit that evening accomplished nothing aside from buoying a little Severn's drooping spirits, and then as night fell there was no sleep for either man. Through the long silence in the candlelit room, Severn sat in a chair by Keats' bed applying a moist cloth to the burning forehead, watching as Keats dozed or awakened to demand angrily that he be given the bottle of laudanum.

At last morning came, but it brought the bleary-eyed Severn only another emergency when Keats was seized by another couching fit, again bringing up blood, frighteningly as much in quantity as the previous day. Again Severn ran for Clark, and again the doctor hurried over and drew off from Keats' arm some eight ounces of blood. More than ever "alarmed and dejected," after Clark left, Keats loudly insisted that he be given the laudanum, and only by much earnest soothing was Severn able to "talk him into a little calmness." Nor was that the finish. For the next three of four mornings renewed coughing instantly produced more blood, less than the two previous attacks but enough to send the sufferer into further raving moods.

Again and again Keats demanded the bottle of laudanum so that he might make a quick end. When Severn refused, he argued that his death was certain and in that case why should his life be prolonged?

Then he tried scaring Severn into compliance by describing in detail what he could expect in tending a man doomed to a wasting death. At last he lost all patience: "On my persistent refusal he grew more and more violent against me, and I was afraid he might die in the midst of his despairing rage." With that, Severn got rid of the bottle by giving it to Dr. Clark, and thereafter Keats became "silent and resigned, and sank into a solemn seriousness." Now, whenever Dr. Clark came over to see his patient, which he did at least once a day, Keats would look up at his entrance and ask wryly, "How long is this posthumous life of mine to last?" (a phrase, interestingly, he'd first used in his last letter to Brown, while he was still in health).

In that hectic week, Severn never went to bed, never removed his clothes for the night, but sat in a chair by the fitfully dozing poet, cooling his forehead and handing him glasses of water. On December 14th, as Keats lay quietly in his bed, Severn began a letter home relaying the devastating news of Keats' shocking collapse. The spasmodic sentences and half-formed thoughts betray a little of his exhaustion:

> My dear Brown,
>
> I fear our poor Keats is at his worst—a most unlooked for relapse has confined him to his bed—with every chance against him: it has been so sudden upon what I almost thought convalescence—and without any seeming cause that I can calculate on the next change. I dread it, for his suffering is so great, so continued, and his fortitude so completely gone, that any further change must make him delirious. This is the fifth day and I see him getting worse. But stop—I will tell you the manner of the relapse from the first

There the letter halts, interrupted from whatever cause, some eruption on the part of Keats, or Severn's own weary inability to get the words down. Through the fifteenth and sixteenth there was no change. His nights Severn spent in a chair soothing Keats' "wanderings," and his days reading and talking to him, never more than a few steps away from the sickbed. It was four o'clock on the morning of

December 17th when, with Keats in a deep sleep—"the first in 8 nights" —Severn stole softly into the other room and again picked up his pen, adding to his unfinished letter of three days before.

The terrible facts of the relapse he recounts in some detail and explains how the small amount of food Keats is allowed leaves him"in perpetual hunger and craving," his digestion so disrupted that he scarcely manages to keep down the little he does eat. Continually he cries out from the gnawing hunger, and "you cannot think how dreadful this is for me—the Doctor on the one hand tells me I shall kill him to give him more than he allows—and Keats raves for more . . ."

Beyond the physical suffering there was Keats' mental state, now deteriorated to the point where the sight of his dull gaze and his muttered talk brings the tears to Severn's eyes:

> . . . I hope he will not wake until I have written this, for I am anxious beyond measure to have you know this worse and worse state—yet I dare not let him see I think it dangerous . . .
>
> His mind is worse than all—despair in every shape—his imagination and memory present every image in horror, so strong that morning and night I tremble for his intellect. The recollection of England—of his "good friend Brown" —his happy few weeks in Mrs. Brawne's Care—his Sister and brother—O he will mourn over every circumstance to me whilst I cool his burning forehead until I tremble through every vein in concealing my tears from his staring glassy eyes . . .
>
> How he can be Keats again from all this I have little hope—but I may see it too gloomy since each coming night I sit up adds its dismal contents to my mind . . .

As for himself, concludes Severn, aside from sheer physical exhaustion, "I will confess my spirits have been sometimes quite pulled down . . . here I am obliged to wash up—cook—and read to Keats all day—added to this I have had no letters yet from my family—this is a damp to me for I never knew how dear they were."

Bravely he finishes, "But if Keats recovers—and then letters bring good news [of his family]—why I shall take it upon myself to be myself again." If, when writing those words, he'd known of one additional fact, he would have felt much less optimistic.

All the excitement on the second floor of No. 26, all Dr. Clark's hastening back and forth, no doubt also the incessant noise of coughing behind closed doors, had alerted the landlady, Signora Angeletti. Perhaps by patient listening in the hallways, or by gossip among other residents in the piazza, she had gained some knowledge of what was transpiring and had promptly made her own diagnosis of the situation. Mr. Keats was not merely ailing, she decided, making a peremptory judgment from which even Dr. Clark still held back, but was actually dying, and from a specific disease, consumption. In such a case, she was well aware, Italian law required an immediate report to the police, and through them to the health authorities. Even had she been well disposed toward her two young tenants, she had no choice. Certainly, also, she felt a good deal of resentment, beyond the dinner-tossing incident, over being deceived into accepting a renter who was seriously ill.

Soon after Severn wrote his letter of December 17th, without a word to anyone, Signora Angeletti went to the police. Another week would pass after that before the hard-pressed Severn heard of the action and learned of some further worries and complications he had in store.

Through the remaining days of December no real improvement occurred in Keats' condition, except that, mercifully, in coughing he ceased to bring up blood. But he remained confined to bed and was kept on almost a starvation diet. Now often weakly feverish, he had grown deathly pale, his eyes glassy, and his mind heavily brooding, as Severn put it, on "the fatal prospect of Consumption." Almost unmoving, he lay in bed turning every thought "to despair and wretchedness . . . the remembrance of his brother's death I cannot keep from him—all his own symptoms he recollects in him."

Most painful of all, his mind dwelt continually on the utter crushing of his hopes for literary achievement, even naming those interminable hours he spent at his desk writing as a contributing cause of his illness. Echoing Keats' words, Severn records that thought in the downright phrase, "the continued stretch of his imagination has killed him, and were he to recover he could not write another line . . . he shakes his head at it all and bids it farewell." Keenly alive to the terrible reality underlying Keats' grieving, the sympathetic Severn cannot help anointing his friend—in obvious sincerity and from intimate knowledge, but speaking with the voice of the younger generation already looking beyond Coleridge and Wordsworth—as the "most noble-feeling and brightest genius to be found in existence."

His angry abandonment made worse by his loss of bodily strength, Keats' personality now underwent a change, bringing on sudden fits of unprovoked nastiness, little incidents of "malevolence," as Severn put it, along with frequent expressions of "suspicion and impatience." Once when Severn made him a cup of coffee, he accepted the cup, then deliberately flung it to the floor, the liquid splashing around. Calmly Severn made another cup and brought it to the glowering patient, who promptly threw it even further across the room. When Severn, still unruffled, brought a third cup, Keats relented and contritely apologized for his "savageness."

Now little disposed to talk, the sick man late on Christmas Eve surprised his companion by bursting out with an unexpected and wholly uncharacteristic comment: "I think a malignant being must have power over us!" Some evil entity, he was sure, had gained control of human affairs, an entity "over whom the Almighty had little or no influence." It was a bit later on that same night that he confessed something that had been troubling him for weeks, his intense spiritual yearning now that he was faced with possible death. "You know, Severn, I can't believe in your book, the bible. But I feel the horrible want of some faith—some hope—something to rest on." For so penetrating an imagination, that shadowy "malignant being" was far too stark, too terrifically hopeless an idea. It needed a counterweight.

There was one book above all, ventured Keats, one book which might help him find some hope, some faith, give him something to rest on, the famous *Holy Dying* of Jeremy Taylor. As Severn discovered, the volume was not easy to find in Rome, but Dr. Clark managed to track down a copy, and every day thereafter, morning and evening, Severn read from its sonorous pages, affording Keats "great comfort" and helping to settle his mind. No mention is made of which parts of Taylor were read out, but much of the book would have been appropriate. For Keats, rather obviously, some of the topics listed in the contents must have had more instant appeal, stirring a mixture of memory, desire, and wan regret. This passage, perhaps, reflecting on how even the shortest life can be wasted:

> We complain that within thirty or forty years, a little more or a great deal less, we shall descend again into the bowels of our Mother, and that our life is too short for any great employment . . . In taking the accounts of your life do not reckon by great distances, and by the periods of pleasure, or the satisfaction of your hopes or the stating your desires . . . he that reckons he hath lived but so many harvests, thinks they come not often enough and that they go away too soon. Some lose the day with longing for the night, and the night in waiting for the day. Hope and fantastic expectations spend much of our lives . . .

Or this passage, which "helps to sweeten the bitter cup of death" by calling over life's woes:

> Man never hath one day to himself of entire peace from the things of this world, but either something troubles him, or nothing satisfies him, or his very fulness swells him and makes him breathe short upon his bed. Men's joys are troublesome, and besides that the fear of losing them takes away the present pleasure . . . They arise from vanity and they dwell upon ice, and they converse with the wind, and they have the wings of a bird, and are serious but as the resolutions of a child . . . as Livius Drusus said of himself, he never had any play days or days of quiet when he was a boy, for he was troublesome and busy, a restless and unquiet man, the same

may every man observe to be true of himself: he is always restless
and uneasy, he dwells upon the waters, and leans upon thorns, and
lays his head upon a sharp stone.

The readings had another, not unusual effect, creating a prayerful
mood in both men and leading to actual prayer sessions, Keats join-
ing in silently at least. Whenever the poet was willing, says Severn, "I
prayed by him and so great a change and calmness grew upon him
that my task was much lightened." A committed practicing Christian,
during these quiet interludes Severn showed much sensitive understanding, being especially careful to avoid even the appearance of
attempting to influence Keats in his beliefs. Not for a moment, he
said, did he "push my little but honest Religious faith upon poor
Keats except as far as my feelings go—but these I try to keep from
him."

After spending the whole night of December 23rd, and into the
next morning, writing letters, at 4:30 A.M. he began still another, his
fifth letter in succession. In it he supplies details of everything that
had happened recently, then brings matters up to the minute:

This is the third week, and I have not left him more than two
hours—he has not been out of bed the whole time—he says this
alone is enough to kill him was he in health . . . sometimes I suc-
ceed in persuading him he will recover and go back with me to
England—I do lament a thousand times that he ever left
England—not from the want of medical aid or even friends, for
nothing can be superior to the kindness of Dr. Clark etc. . . . but
the journey of 2000 miles was too much . . .

For myself my dear Sir—I still keep up nearly as well as I did—
altho' I have not got any person to relieve me—Keats makes me
careful of myself—he is my doctor—a change of scene might
make me better, but I can do without it. It is 6 oclock in the Morg.
I have been writing all night—this is my 5th letter—Keats has just
awoken—I must leave off and boil my kettle . . .

Ending his letter, Severn mentions that Keats has heard the scratching of his quill on the paper and asked who he was writing to. Told that it was John Taylor, the publisher, Keats came back with a pun appropriate to a bookman, making a joke of his own uncertain fate: "Tell Taylor I shall soon be in a second Edition—in sheets—and cold press." A calm mind, indeed, again with some balance. The incident illustrates a relevant fact of Keats' last days, that even when things were at their worst he could still flash out with something of his old humor. As Severn wrote later, "With all his suffering and consciousness of approaching death, he never quite lost the play of his cheerful and elastic mind."

That same afternoon Severn resumed the letter, and was just finishing it when a note from Dr. Clark was brought to the door. It carried the devastating information about Signora Angeletti's trip to the police station. Not wanting even to think about the possiblity of Keats' death, refusing to accept the necessity of the commonsense precautions of the Italian health code, he angrily reached for his finished letter and, cross-writing, on the third page added a heated paragraph:

4 oclock. This moment the doctor sends me word that my Landlady has reported to the Police that Keats is dying of a Consumption—now this has made me vent some curses against her—the words dying and Consumption have rather damped my spirits—the laws are very severe—I do not know the extent of them—should poor Keats die, everything in his room is condemned to be burned even to the paper on the walls. The Italians are so alarmed at Consumption that the expenses are enormous after a death—for examinations and precautions to contagion—Fools. I can hardly contain myself. O! I will be revenged on this old Cat—for putting the notion in my head of my friends dying . . .

Severn might continue to reject the diagnosis of full-blown consumption and to hope for a recovery of some sort for a very good reason. Dr. Clark himself was not even yet ready to admit the presence of actual tuberculosis. The coughed-up blood, he thought, had probably come from ruptured vessels in the disorganized stomach, if not the stressed lungs, a result of "a total derangement of the digestive powers," by then weakened so far as to be almost nonoperative. While Clark much feared it would not be long before consumption did set in, he also felt that a drastic alteration in the patient's mental attitude could still work a thorough healing. If he could bring his ragged emotions under control, Keats might even now get better.

On the other hand, the realistic Clark admitted to having very little real hope that this would happen. "Poor fellow . . . his stomach is still in a very bad state, the affection of his lungs is increasing and the state of his mind is the most deplorable possible." An added reason for the emotional setback just at this time was the arrival of a letter from Fanny, apparently her first to the poet since he left home. It arrived in a batch of five that reached No. 26 a few days before Christmas, two for Severn, three for Keats. His first two Keats perused with interest, but Fanny's he put down unread—either before opening it or after he'd had a glance at the familiar hand—fearful of coming across some unthinking word or phrase that would reawaken his jealous suspicions. His mood as he put her letter aside, reported the watching Severn, was one of deep dejection: "He was effected most bitterly."

But if he would not read Fanny's letter (he may, of course, have read it when alone in his room, that day or later), he had another, different means of bringing her vividly to mind, the oval carnelian she'd given him when parting in Hampstead. This polished little stone, according to Severn, he held "continually in his hand . . . at times it seemed his only consolation, the only thing left him in this world clearly tangible." Warmed in his palm, it would in its own peculiar way have helped promote the serenity he so much needed, a serenity that might easily be blasted by some unguarded phrase or expression surprising him in a letter.

The mood lasted through Christmas—the dreariest Christmas he'd ever spent, said the downcast Severn—and then into the first days of the new year. Increasingly during that time Severn's unrelenting burden made itself felt—his many nursing chores, including constant reading aloud, coupled with lack of sleep, had their inevitable effect on his nerves. During one especially low point he can be heard making a pitiful bid for sympathy in one of his letters to his family: "I light the fire, make his breakfast, & sometimes am obliged to cook—make his bed and even sweep the room. I can have these things done, but never at the time when they ought and must be done." What enraged him most of all, he said, was the simple task of making a fire. "I blow—blow—for an hour—the smoke comes fuming out—my kettle falls over on the burning sticks—no stove—Keats calling me to be with him—the fire catching my hands and the doorbell ringing." Sheepishly, as if apologizing for the brief show of self-indulgence, he reminds his correspondent of his fumbling unfitness for such work: "All these to one quite unused and not at all capable."

But then, unexpectedly, taking even Dr. Clark by surprise, Keats began to brighten. Visibly his spirits lifted, his face began getting back some color, his eyes took on their old eager look, and a smile, perhaps a bit wan, returned to his lips. Astonished and delighted, Severn soon resolved to help the improvement along by affording Keats a little change of scene, still within the apartment. After lying so long in the cramped bedroom, the sick man needed something to look at besides the rows of rosettes dotting the ceiling, so Severn moved him during the day to the sofa in the sitting room. Mindful of the health code requirements, however, he took care that no one but Dr. Clark knew of the transfer, even blocking the door with furniture while Keats was on the sofa. The furnishings in the sitting room were worth, Severn estimated, several thousand dollars, and in the case of a death by consumption every piece would have to be destroyed, himself being liable for the cost.

The improvement in Keats seemed to proceed from no specific cause. But Severn thought he knew better than that, knew that it was at least partly a happy result of the sessions with the soothing influence of Jeremy Taylor's *Holy Dying*, as well as the quiet prayers of the two men (Keats at least silently joined in the praying of the devout

Severn). Years later Severn recalled how the act of turning Keats' mind away from brooding over his ill luck and lifting it into the realm of the spiritual produced important results. He described how he'd often read the Taylor volume to Keats, "and prayed with him, and I could tell by the grasp of his dear hand that his mind was reviving . . . it did not seem to require much effort in him to embrace the Holy Spirit." The effect on Keats was exactly what Dr. Clark said was needed, something with power to calm that ever-restless mind.

But the physical improvement resulting from the unaccustomed calm did not flow from or point to an imminent recovery. It was something just the opposite.

Paradoxically, in an excited letter written on January 11th, Severn sees the change in Keats as a promise of recovery precisely because he has resigned himself to dying, in this curious way gaining the serenity of acceptance. The letter is addressed to Mrs. Brawne but of course was meant equally for her daughter:

> . . . among all the horrors hovering over our poor Keats this was the most dreadful, that I could see no possible way, and but a fallacious hope for his recovery. But now thank God I have a real one. I most certainly think I shall bring him back to England—at least my anxiety for his recovery and comfort make me think this— . . . he has changed to calmness & quietude, as singular as productive of good, for his mind was certainly killing him. He has now given up all thoughts, hopes or even wish for recovery—his mind is in a state of peace from the final leave he has taken of this world and all its future hopes. This has been an immense weight for him to rise from. He remains quiet and submissive under his heavy fate.
>
> Now if anything will recover him it is this absence of himself. I have perceived for the last three days symptoms of recovery—Dr. Clark even thinks so—Nature again revives in him . . .

He adds what he knows Mrs. Brawne will like to hear, that both the doctor and his good-hearted wife show the greatest concern not only for Keats but for himself as well. "I can't tell which shows us the most kindness. *I* am even a mark of their care—mince pies and numberless nice things come over to keep me alive—and but for their kindness I am afraid we should go on very gloomily."

Signing his name he put down his pen, then took a candle and tiptoed into the darkened bedroom. Holding the candle high, he saw that Keats beneath the blanket lay in a deep slumber, breathing easily. He returned to his desk and beneath the signature added:

I have just looked at him—he is in a beautiful sleep—in look he is very much more himself—I have the greatest hopes for him—

The change in the personality of Fanny Brawne, her maturing from a mixture of girlish fear and giddiness to womanly self-possession, began at Wentworth Place on the morning of the tenth of January, 1820. Its precipitating cause was the startling news, brought to the Brawnes by Brown, of Keats' blood-drenched relapse the previous month. For the first time seriously, young Fanny came face to face with the possibility that the man she loved might actually die.

Severn's dual letter of December 14th-17th reached London on January 9th. In graphic terms it told of Keats' renewed dire suffering, while making the doleful admission that he was "at his worst . . . with every chance against him," that his condition was "dangerous," and that even if he survived there existed little hope that "he can be Keats again from all this."

Anticipating the awful effect such stark news would have on the girl, Brown hesitated to show the letter next door. But after a night of thinking things over, he determined to inform at least Mrs. Brawne, leaving it to her whether Fanny should be told the truth, and how much. This he did on the following day ("Mrs. Brawne was greatly agitated when I told her") and as he soon learned, she promptly gave her daughter the full truth, allowing her to read Severn's letter as well. "She bears it with great firmness," wrote Brown a bit cryptically, "mournfully but without affectation." He meant, it seems, that while she didn't give much outward sign of worry, her accustomed bright-ness was considerably subdued, an interpretation borne out by later evidence.

But Brown also learned that Fanny's *first* reaction to the news had been quite the opposite of subdued, her inexperienced heart plung-ing to the extreme of outright despair. "I believe he must soon die!" she cried to her mother. "When you hear of his death tell me imme-diately." Rather fiercely she added, as if to claim a maturity she knew she lacked, "I am not a fool!" If later readers have missed the true import of those words, so familiar in the mouths of the young, the sympathetic Mrs. Brawne did not. She knew that in reality they were a cry, not clearly recognized by her young daughter, that said, Yes, I *have* been a fool at times, but shall be so no longer!

Ten days of anxious waiting passed, and then another letter arrived from Rome (that of December 24th). It reported that, while the hem-orrhaging had ceased, and Keats' digestion was better, matters remained "quite as hopeless" as before. The specter of consumption for Keats "turns everything to despair and wretchedness, he will not bear the idea of living much less strive to live." This letter also made its way to the Brawnes, and no doubt into Fanny's trembling hands.

There intervened another agonized stretch of waiting, with the terrible expectation of Keats' momentary death hovering over the London circle. Then on February 1st Severn's letter to Mrs. Brawne arrived, with its almost gleeful announcement of new hope: "I most certainly think I shall bring him back to England." Interestingly, however, those joyful words failed to have their full effect on Fanny. To her (but not to her mother who said that Severn's news "cheers us"), the enthusiastic portrayal by Severn of his reason for elation—Keats' resigning himself to death—seemed egregiously self-contra-dictory.

But in this there is no need to quote Fanny at second or third hand. Here at last the young woman, up to now seen only through Keats' eyes, moves to center stage and may speak for herself and in her own voice.

On the first of February, only two hours after the arrival of Severn's letter to her mother, Fanny began a letter of her own, to Keats' sister, in which she brings the sixteen-year-old up to date on the poet's condition. Not easy to picture in the flow of earnest words is the fashionable, at times rather flighty young thing so eager to turn men's heads at parties, the socializing charmer who was happy only when receiving a compliment.

Before this, in writing Keats' sister, Fanny had deliberately, and perhaps on the advice of her mother, withheld the bad news received earlier:

My Dear Girl,

I have been this week wishing to write to you but putting it off everyday in hopes of having something concerning your brother to communicate which would not give you pain, but it is in vain to wait any longer. Oh my dear, he is very ill, he has been so ever since the 8th of December.

If I had written this letter two hours sooner I should have owned to you that I had scarcely a hope remaining and even now when I have just received a letter from Mr Severn with the nearest approaching to good news that we have had since this last attack, there is nothing to rest upon, merely a hope, a chance.

But I will tell you all in as collected a way as I can. On the 10th of January Mr Brown received a letter from Rome saying your brother had been attacked with spitting of blood and that the symptoms were very bad. He had been ill for 17 days and did not appear to get better. I judged of you by myself and though I was then about to write I deferred it for some time in hopes a letter more cheering might arrive. I cannot think I was wrong.

If you knew how much I regretted that it had not been kept from me—how continually I thought a fortnight or even a week's ignorance of it would have been more pain spared—and when at last I could not bear to keep silence any longer for fear you should fancy the least neglect should have occasioned it, I wrote a letter that without mentioning anything positively bad, did not, if I may judge from your answer, give you hopes of a speedy recovery.

Once or twice we have heard slight accounts, which were neither calculated to raise or depress our hope but yesterday I was told of a letter from the Physician which said he was exactly the same. He did not get better nor did he get worse. But could I conceal from myself that with him, not getting better was getting worse? If ever I gave up hope, I gave it up then. I tried to destroy it, I tried to persuade myself that I should never see him again. I felt that you ought no longer to remain in ignorance and the whole of this day I have been thinking how I could tell you. I am glad, very glad, I waited, for I have just received the account I spoke of in the beginning of this letter.

Mr Severn says that for the first time he feels a hope, he thinks he shall bring him back to us. Surely that is saying a great deal—and yet the reason he gives for that hope destroys it, [namely] for the last 3 days (the letter was dated the 11th of Jan) your brother had been calm, he had resigned himself to die.

Oh can you bear to think of it, he had given up even wishing to live—Good God! is it to be borne that he, formed for everything good, and, I think I dare say it, for everything great, is to give up his hopes of life and happiness, so young too . . . I am sure nothing during his long illness has hurt me so much as to hear that he was resigned to die.

. . . my dear Sister, for so I feel you to be, forgive me if I have not sufficiently softened this wretched news. Indeed I am not able to contrive words that would appear less harsh—if I am to lose him I lose everything and then you, after my Mother will be the only person I feel interest or attachment for—I feel that I love his sister as my own . . .

Despite its being composed under a degree of emotional pressure, despite Fanny's obvious concern, the letter is supremely interesting for what can be read beneath the surface.

Pass over as perhaps inadvertent the curious slighting in that last sentence of her own sister and brother. Pass over as well the contradiction between Fanny's insisting earlier that she be told even the worst news as soon as it was known ("I am not a fool!") and her wish here that the bad news had been kept from her, sparing her pain. What can't be passed over is the way she remains wholly unaffected by Severn's apparent good news of January 11th.

Strangely, she looks past the fact that Severn is on the scene in Rome and has been observing Keats for many weeks, looks past the fact that Dr. Clark also sees in the patient evident signs of a recovery. She is impressed only by what appears to her a contradiction: how can anyone be saved by a willingness to die? Yet Severn's reasoning is correct, for resignation in any difficult situation *does* bring a certain peace of mind, a calming of mental turmoil, often deeply so, just the result needed by the troubled poet. It is Fanny's own peculiar quality of interior aloofness—*disjunction* may describe it better—which kept her from finding an occasion for joy in Severn's optimistic letter. It was that same disjunction which kept her from appreciating, really caring about, Keats' severe resentment of her coquettish ways.

Quite evidently, Fanny has been profoundly moved and bothered by one particular aspect of Severn's report, the disturbing fact that Keats had "given up even wishing to live." The poet's despairing surrender, obscuring all else, grips her whole attention, wringing from her a confession that "nothing during his long illness has hurt me so much as to hear that he was resigned to die." It is the phrase *hurt me* in that sentence which tells most, for the poet's willingness to die is a recurrent note in the letters he wrote Fanny, at times becoming an outright desire for death. Surely it is no very wild suggestion to say that Fanny, during the terrible weeks of waiting for further news to arrive from Rome, took out those thirty-nine or more letters, achingly going over each page, each line, remembering.

If she had not specially noticed it before, she certainly did so now, Keats' peculiar affinity for the idea of death, his fondness for picturing his own demise, pursued both as habit and with deliberation. There was his awkwardly glib remark about having "two luxuries to brood over in my walks, your Loveliness and the hour of my death."

There was his youthfully flippant and offensive wish to leave the world by taking "a sweet poison from your lips," for which she'd reprimanded him. More to the point now were his random comments about the corrosive effect on him of her loose conduct toward men.

If she continued to behave badly, he'd written in one letter, "I do not want to live . . . I wish this coming night may be my last," and for that same reason he hoped that his eyes might close "on their last repose." Worst by far were the piercing phrases he'd penned in his farewell letter to her after echoing Hamlet's charge against inconstant women. "I should like to give the matter up at once," he cries. "I should like to die . . . I am sickened at the brute world which you are smiling with . . . I am glad there is such a thing as the grave—I am sure I shall never have any rest till I get there."

Poor, youthful, confused Fanny, having at such a time to look back on such a bitter complaint, and having to admit that it was she who had prompted it.

SIX

TO CEASE AT MIDNIGHT

In his hand Dr. Clark held a thin wooden tube about a foot long. At the top no more than half an inch in diameter, it subtly widened along its length, at the other end flaring to the shape of a small bugle-mouth. Stretched on the bed beneath the covers, bare to the waist, lay Keats. Delicately, Clark touched the flared end of the tube to the chest, bent down and put his ear to the other end, then listened. Over the next fifteen minutes he moved the tube to several other locations on the chest, listening, then had the patient turn over. Carefully he repeated the procedure on the broad back.

A day or two afterward, on January 15th, Joseph Severn recorded the fact that the nature of Keats' ailment had finally been settled. The presence of the dread consumption, he wrote in a letter home, had been "confirmed." Keats' recovery and the rising hope that he might after all be able to surmount his illness had lasted hardly two weeks.

The use of a stethoscope in its earliest form on Keats cannot be proved, but it is strongly indicated by the circumstances, and Clark of course was among the first to be familiar with its use. No further hemorrhaging had occurred, nor had any fresh symptoms of any sort appeared. Only two days previous Clark had still been unsure of his diagnosis. Without the new instrument there was simply no means by which Clark at that time could have reached so definite a conclusion, no way he might have "confirmed" the consumption.

Severn gives as "proofs" of the confirmation five conditions: continual production of phlegm not always streaked with blood, a dry cough, night sweats, wasting of flesh, and "great uneasiness in the chest." But the first four conditions were not new and by themselves would never have convinced Clark (the dry cough and heavy production of phlegm, in any case, seem a contradiction). It must have been the "uneasiness" in the chest cavity that persuaded him, the peculiar, tell-tale rasping sound of the lungs in breathing, made loud and distinguishable by the magic of the thin wooden tube. Severn was probably present at the examination, but his not mentioning a stethoscope means little. Knowing nothing of medical instruments, new or old, he would have taken it for granted. In fact, at the same time, Clark had tried another means of reaching a diagnosis, bringing in a specialist, an Italian physician (he suggested that Keats was also suffering from some unspecified type of chest malformation). Perhaps it was the Italian doctor who thought of employing a stethoscope.

But whether by means of the newest medical device, or through old-fashioned informed guessing (the proper name for much medical diagnosis in the early nineteenth century), Dr. Clark had given his verdict. As was expected, he also supplied a prognosis, something he'd avoided doing before. It was now a matter of weeks, he informed the dismayed Severn, perhaps as little as two or three, and the poet would be facing his end (a certainty of calculation which in itself points to stethoscopic examination).

For Severn, the finality of the pronouncement came with shattering force, producing a turmoil of emotions, first concerning the doomed Keats and then himself. For days his state of mind showed plainly in his drawn face, his subdued voice, and slumping carriage. "I can see under your quiet look," he quotes Keats as saying from his bed one day when he was reading aloud, "immense twisting and contending. What is it puzzles you?" Keats had not been told the full extent of Clark's verdict, so Severn, wishing to avoid the topic, gave an evasive answer. But within a day or two he found some release by pouring his woes into a letter to his friend Haslam.

"I have the veriest load of care that ever came upon these shoulders of mine," he wrote, explaining that he was now faced with the prospect of a huge financial obligation. Aside from some immediate money difficulties (he'd had to pay out his "last solitary Crown" for rent, a situation that was soon cleared up through London), he would be personally liable, after Keats was gone, for repaying the cost of the destroyed furniture and effects from the apartment. This, he knew, could amount to thousands of dollars especially if Signora Angeletti discovered that the sick man had also spent time in the large sitting room. That was bad enough, but "this noble fellow lying on the bed is dying in horror—no kind hope smoothing down his suffering—no philosophy—no religion to support him, yet with all the most gnawing desire for it." Once again the dying man had been crying out for spiritual solace, in words that tore Severn's "very heartstrings." This time he was not asking, but demanding to know why *he* had been singled out as unworthy, why *he* had been left to face his end alone and unprepared.

Through chattering teeth, says Severn, Keats in great distress called out a few fragmentary phrases of almost angry supplication. In truth, and in sober reality, those phrases amount to nothing less than an actual if largely unconscious prayer:

> Miserable wretch I am—this last cheap comfort which every rogue and fool have—is deny'd me in my last moments—why is this—O! I have served everyone with my utmost good—yet why is this—I cannot understand this . . .

Always I have tried to live a good life, Keats is saying, yet here I am dying overcome by doubt and fear and in utter misery of spirit. Why is God doing this awful thing, depriving me of the final comfort he grants to so many! (How familiar a cry that is, how much it resembles the earnest petition voiced by the father of the possessed boy to Jesus, "I believe, help thou my unbelief!") In response, the appalled Severn could only offer to read some passages from Jeremy Taylor's *Holy Dying*. In his letter he added a fervent, obviously sincere hope "that some angel of goodness will lead him through this dark wilderness."

The question of whether Keats—a poet at the same time both pagan and godly—on his deathbed came back to the faith he had disdained as a freethinking teenager (becoming, if anything precisely, a Deist) cannot now be settled. The question remains, though, tantalizing as ever, still eliciting a cacaphony of opinion. One biographer will imperiously dismiss the very possibility, another will say it is unlikely or extremely improbable. Very few are willing to concede that it might have happened, that Keats in his last hours might have turned back to the faith of his youth.

Robert Gittings, one of the ablest of Keats' chroniclers, briefly reviews the evidence, then concludes that everything said by Severn on the topic, early and late, was simply "to persuade himself that Keats had died a Christian." The poet certainly did, Gittings agrees, become "more reconciled" to his fate at the end, but there is "no sign that he accepted any of the comforts of his friend's Christianity." What Gittings *means* to say is clear, of course, but he has not quite said it, showing how hard it can be when treating this question to keep the scales in balance. *Some* of the comforts of Christianity, Keats certainly did accept, and with gratitude, namely, the spiritual insights provided by Bishop Jeremy Taylor. During many weeks before his death, Keats listened attentively to Severn reading from the pages of *Holy Dying*, often twice a day, morning and evening. (Did Severn in answer to Keats' unconscious prayer read the section entitled, "Of the practice of the grace of faith in time of sickness," or another called, "Of repentance in time of sickness" ? Perhaps Keats himself would have preferred to hear "Consideration of the Vanity and shortness of man's life," or a briefer comment on "The miseries of man's life").

Certainly Keats gave no definite sign of conversion, none that has entered the record. Yet there is one other small bit of evidence to be considered, one that has never been given its due weight, that is, the good example set by Severn's tireless service on behalf of his friend during those long months in Rome. Keats knew very well that what his companion was doing for him was something out of the ordinary, knew that Severn was risking both his artistic future and his health (the interminable sleepless nights and the unrelenting daily attention, if nothing else). It puzzled him to explain why and how so young a man, with so much of his own life to live, could do so much so uncomplainingly. Then the answer dawned.

"Severn," said Keats suddenly one day, "I now understand how you can bear all this—'Tis your Christian faith; and here am I, with desperation in death that would disgrace the commonest fellow!" It is correct, of course, that Severn's religious faith played its large part in enabling him to carry the strain (he said so himself), nor was it the first time that example spoke so loudly. Keats' not only seeing the truth but putting it into words must not be lightly passed over. He'd been given, it appears, rather more than a nudge toward reconciliation.

In later years Severn occasionally reverted to the question of Keats' spiritual hunger in those last hours. Once in an article published in 1863 in both England and America, he recalled how it had been with Keats during those pathetic final days at No. 26: "In all he then uttered he breathed a simple, Christian spirit; indeed I always think that he died a Christian, that 'Mercy,' was trembling on his dying lips, and that his tortured soul was received by those Blessed Hands which could alone welcome it." In that belated statement a reader may place as much or as little credence as he wishes—taking care to note Severn's own judicious "I always think," which rightly does not insist on the accuracy of his opinion. But concerning one additional fact, since it was reported at the time by the man who witnessed it, there is no argument. In his last hours when the suffering Keats felt that death was hovering only hours away, more than once he murmured a heartfelt *Thank God*!

※

By the end of January 1821, his own personal affairs had begun to weigh heavily on Severn, and he was especially worried about getting his Academy picture finished. Weeks had gone by in which he hadn't picked up a brush, probably the planned painting hadn't even been completely sketched out. He had also begun to feel the delayed effects of his six weeks' night-and-day nursing, a grueling period in which hardly for a moment had he breathed the air outside the cramped apartment. Now his prospects for a rest seemed even more remote. But even as he thought longingly of getting some relief, he was held back by a feeling of guilt at the idea of deserting his charge. "I will not give myself a jot of credit unless I stand firm," he wrote Haslam, "and will too. You'd be rejoiced to see how I am kept up—not a flinch yet. I read—cook—make the beds and do all the menial offices, for no soul comes near Keats except the doctor and myself."

Brave words, and he more than lived up to them, never letting his sick friend know how difficult life had become for him. But cresting now in Severn's youthful heart was a rising desire for the carefree existence he'd known in London, especially the warmth and joy he'd always found among his own large family. On the evening of Sunday, January 21st, with Keats asleep in the other room, he sat down at a candlelit table to take a solitary supper. Propped in front of him was a picture, a small group painting on ivory he'd made before leaving England: father, mother, three sisters, and two brothers, all heads and shoulders cleverly lined up sideways in a row. Waiting for his meal to arrive in the basket from the *trattoria*, while looking at the picture he began writing a letter home. The loving portrait he draws of the family circle, and his own accustomed place in it, shows how strong was his need for some respite from the physical and emotional strain of the past weeks:

> Away from you all I feel my sundays pass the heaviest. Today is going drearily so I will sit down and dine with your pictures, for my only real pleasure is the remembrance of you all. Here it passes in my mind.
> "Is Joseph come?"
> "Why he always comes when dinner is over."

"Ah!" says my poor Mother (Heaven preserve her to see all my views accomplished and in them myself happy), "Ah! and all the nice cabbage cold."

"Yes!" says my father, "drat the young dog. Are you sure Charles he said he'd come?"

"O yes, he was all ready. I left him—"

"O here he is, here he is!"

See the conquering hero comes, peel your turnips, pick your plums, wines prepare and dishes bring, round the table make a ring, see the dog's-tail Joseph advance. But I cannot be merry unless I be with you, yet this train of thought always helps me to be happy.

O! the English welcome I always had at my dear father's table, the kind and loving faces I always saw, the happy contented look of my father when I visited him, and the oftener the more happy he seemed. The anxious tender look of my mother with all her kind inquiries, then the good-natured laugh of my dear Maria, and her eye looking at me from head to foot to see that her Joseph was all neat and clean. Hearty Tom looking at me and at some new music at once, eating his dinner and playing on the organ at the same time.

O! this is woven round and round my heart . . .

After he'd jotted a few more sentences the dinner arrived, and he put the letter aside, intending to add to it when he could. Another three weeks would pass, however, before he again had a quiet moment in which to write letters to anyone. The brooding Keats was now at his lowest, grown morose and loudly irritable by turns, a condition that again demanded Severn's whole attention.

From his bed Keats would growl at Severn that he no longer cared for books and wanted to have none near him. Severn must clear them all out of his room, every last one. Then a few days later he would reverse himself, directing that all the many books in the apartment be piled on and around his bed. Another day he'd be talking of his early life, something he seldom did when well, his tone earnest and melancholy. Then his mood would again shift, this time to loud, indignant anger as he berated the startled Severn for keeping the bottle of lau-danum from him. He'd meant to take it, he said, the instant he felt his recovery was impossible. The sleepless nights of fevered sweating and endless painful coughing he couldn't face, he declared fiercely, and above all did not wish to be a witness "to the wasting of his body."

For keeping him alive against his will, raved Keats at his friend, no punishment, no privation would be too much. Then would come silence as Keats, subdued once more, stared from his bed at the hag-gard Severn, feeling sudden concern at the look of extreme fatigue that darkened the face always before so brightly smiling. A nurse must be engaged, Keats would insist, to come in every day and give Severn a chance to get some fresh air and exercise. Eventually the ser-vices of a nurse, an Italian woman (who probably spoke no English), were arranged. On January 26th she reported for duty only to have Keats, again in a black mood, petulantly wave her off. She wouldn't do, explained Severn in a letter, because there were so many things Keats wanted done "that no one can do but myself." Feeling a little better, he had determined to keep on alone in the apartment, he said, "without any more going out. Keats is wanting to say something or have something done every minute in the day."

Ending his letter, he adds a nervous comment which shows that Keats' bad temper at this period was in some degree actual delirium, though Severn saw it as worse than that: "I can assure you his mind is bordering on the insane . . . the strangeness of his mind everyday surprises us—no one feeling or notion like any other being." When Keats, still delirious, began refusing food, perhaps thinking to starve himself to death, Severn had a struggle to persuade him otherwise. Often he painstakingly prepared a half-dozen different little meals the same day, a variety intended to leave the patient "no excuse."

As the new year dawned, Severn's lonely nighttime vigils went on, either in a chair at the patient's bedside or hunched over his desk in the other room as he kept himself awake by writing letters. Fighting drowsiness in the small bedroom, lit by a single shielded candle, often he would nod off while sitting in a chair. Once in the small hours

No. 26 Piazza di Spagna, beside
the Spanish Steps. Keats' room is
at the corner on the third floor
(two above the ground floor).
Bernini's boat-fountain in
 foreground.

Pencil sketch of Joseph
Severn made in 1822, the year
after Keats' death (Seymour
Kirkup, artist).

Keats at age 23 (1818) in a miniature oil on ivory by Severn (detail).
When Keats went to Rome hoping to recover his health, the original
was given to Fanny Brawne.

Three views of Fanny Brawne: silhouette by Edouart, 1829; painted miniature of about 1830, artist unknown; ambrotype of about 1850, which shows her after some twenty years of marriage and the birth of three children.

Tuesday Morn.

My dearest Girl,

I wrote a letter for you yesterday expecting to have seen your mother. I shall be selfish enough to send it though I know it may give you a little pain, because I wish you to see how unhappy I am for love of you, and endeavour as much as I can to entice you to give up your whole heart to me whose whole existence hangs upon you. You could not step or move an eyelid but it would shoot to my heart — I am greedy of you. Do not think of any thing but me. Do not live as if I was not existing. Do not forget me — But have I any right to say you forget me? Perhaps you think of me all day. Have I any right to wish you to be unhappy for me? You would forgive me for wishing it, if you knew the extreme passion I have that you should love me. and for you to love me as I do you, you must think of no one but me, much less write that sentence. Yesterday and this morning I have been haunted with a sweet vision

Letter of Keats to Fanny Brawne, written in June 1819. With it he enclosed the letter written to her "yesterday . . . though I know it may give you a little pain." For a discussion of these letters see the text, 58-65.

Keats' room at No. 26 Piazza di Spagna as it is preserved today. The bed on which he died would have been placed opposite the fireplace (mantle visible on right). The two windows are behind and to the left of the camera.

Dr James Clark, the English doctor who attended Keats in Rome. He served also as a good friend to both Keats and the overworked Severn.

Joseph Severn (left) in the only known photograph of him, taken in Rome. The date is about 1875, some fifty years after Keats' death.

The Piazza di Spagna some hundred years afer Keats' death. The Keats house, No. 26, is the first on the left. At center foreground is the Bernini fountain.

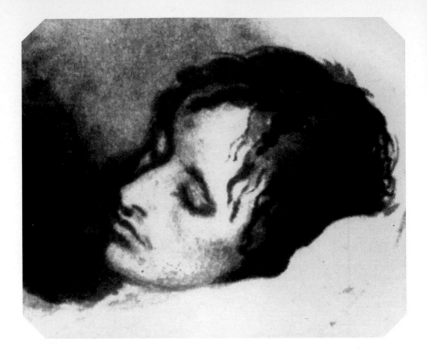

(Above) pencil sketch made by Joseph Severn in the lamplight at the bedside of the dying Keats. (Below) neighboring tombstones of Keats and Severn in the Protestant Cemetary, Rome.

toward dawn, with the gentle plashing of the Bernini fountain drifting up through the darkness, he kept himself alert by doing a sketch of the sleeping Keats. The head, propped up on pillows to make breathing easier, shows a face with eyes peacefully closed, a face still full, smooth, and strangely unravaged by disease. But the disheveled hair straggling over the forehead is matted against the skin, signaling that this is not untroubled sleep. Finishing the sketch, Severn jotted along the bottom of the sheet, "28 January—3 o'clock morng—drawn to keep me awake—a deadly sweat was on him all this night."

Early February brought little change in the dreary routine at No. 26. Sometimes Keats would again show himself agitated, angry, bitter, then would grow calmer, talking quietly so that it almost seemed he was enjoying some ease of both body and mind. At such moments, against all reason, Severn even found himself again hoping, almost believing, that his friend would somehow improve, would somewhere find the strength to halt the decline. But each time he attempted to broach the idea to Clark, to draw from the wary doctor some slight indication of agreement, Clark simply "shook his head." Keats, too, now violently rejected even a slight wish for improvement. To him the mere thought of recovery had become "beyond everything dreadful . . . he talks of the quiet grave." The end, Clark confided, was now only a matter of days. Death would surely come by the middle of the month or soon after.

It was now clear to everyone that Severn, if he was to avoid illness himself, needed relief. The sculptor, young Ewing, had occasionally come in to spell him at the sick bed for an hour or so, but a more regular arrangement was required. Accordingly another effort was made at locating a nurse, and this time Dr. Clark was able to find an English woman, one whom Keats fortunately liked. She was available, however, only on a limited basis, being free to come in mornings every other day for two hours. Little as this was it gave the overworked Severn a chance to "run out for a mouthful of fresh air." The nurse's first day on duty was February 4th, a Sunday. In place of an airing, Severn chose work, locking himself in his little painting room where he spent his free two hours with his brushes.

The figure of Fanny Brawne made its last appearance on the scene at Rome on Saturday, February 10th, unfortunately even now not bringing peace. On that day a letter from her to Keats arrived enclosed in a letter from Brown. Breaking the wax seal and undoing the folds of the Brown letter, Keats found the smaller letter inside and before realizing what it was began reading. "The glance of that letter tore him to pieces," recalled Severn, "the effects were on him for many days! He did not read it—he could not, but requested me to place it in his coffin." Hastily, Severn took the offending sheet from Keats' trembling hand and put it aside, but that didn't conclude the disagreeable episode. After that, several days went by and then, suddenly and openly, without the least urging or invitation, Keats began talking to Severn of Fanny, confiding in him in a way he'd never done with anyone, not even in the unguarded nighttime session the day after the landing in Naples. His old doubts again strongly stirred, he complained of her behavior, this time going the length of blaming her for having been a main cause of his illness.

The passage in which Severn records the fact of that conversation occurs in a letter to Brown, written an hour or so later that same day. Brief yet explicit, it follows immediately after the information about Fanny's unexpected letter and leaves no doubt of what the agitated poet said: "he found many causes of his illness in the exciting and thwarting of his passions, but I persuaded him to feel otherwise on this delicate point." In apparent anger, Keats ended by altering his instructions about disposition of the letter: "he has requested me *not* to place that letter in his coffin" (the underlining is Severn's).

What arguments were used by Severn to "persuade" Keats that Fanny shouldn't be held accountable would be interesting to know—how and why in so personal a matter he *presumed* to disagree, even more so. Just possibly the answer lies in the interpretation given by some critics to the word "passions." In those days the open and common use of the term almost always referred to the emotions. But here Keats may indeed have been citing, in some part, not emotional turmoil but sexual frustration, arousal and denial during his sessions with Fanny. That sense does seem to fit a little better with Severn's use of the word "delicate." In that case, Severn would perhaps have felt freer to intervene, and in some measure he appears to have been convincing. Concerning what was to be done with Fanny's letter, he was also able to alter Keats' decision, for he later stated that he placed the letters (adding another that came later) in the coffin "with my own hand."

It was in this same grueling period, Severn recalled, marked as it was by rapid physical deterioration, that the sick man felt most keenly all that he was losing in the literary realm—his chance to gain enrollment high on his country's role of the great. Having now, as he knew, grown far beyond his models, aware of vastly increased technical abilities, conscious of broadening human insight, he was intensely conscious of what he might accomplish with longer life, felt it with absolute certainty in his bones. Is there in any walk of life a deeper, bitterer personal agony than that, to be young and to believe that you are one of the elect while facing the certainty that you will not live to achieve your destiny?

It was that fixed assurance of his latent powers that underlay one of his last outbursts, a rueful remark apparently not quite understood by Severn in his reporting of it.

In mid-February, coming back to the apartment from his usual morning's errand to fetch the milk, Severn told Keats delightedly that he'd spotted some trees beginning to blossom. It looked as if it would be an early spring! But from the prostrate Keats came no answering delight. Instead, the news "had a most dreadful effect on him—I had mistaken the point." As Severn watched in acute discomfort, the fevered, sunken eyes suddenly filled with tears. "Ah! why did you let me know this?" objected Keats wanly. "Why show me that this comfort is gone, that I'll never see the spring again! I hoped to die before it came. O, I would to God that I were in my grave—quiet and insensible to these ghastly hands, these knobbed knees!"

But the distress didn't arise from the bodily wasting, frightening as that was. The hands become clawlike from loss of flesh, the bony knees enlarged by contrast with the thinning thighs and calves, he could have borne. It was the spring, with its bursting array of flowers—"always enchantment to me"—and its radiant renewal of hope, that he couldn't face, not again. He'd had enough of hoping. Now the coming of spring only made him piercingly aware of all he'd be losing.

"The grave—with flowers on its top—send me to it now," he murmured as the crestfallen Severn listened helplessly.

As early as Christmas Eve, Keats had said that he wanted his death to pass in utter silence, to be wholly unnoticed. Not the least mention should "be made of him in any manner publically—in reviews, magazines, or newspapers," and no engraving should be made "from any picture of him." Three weeks after that, talking with Severn on the night of February 14th, he went further. On his tombstone, he instructed, nothing personal should appear, not his name, not his dates. Instead, he wished to have graven on the stone one short line, "Here lies one whose name was writ in water." Severn, relating the touching moment to Brown, says that he knows Brown will understand the line so well that he need say no more. Then he glumly adds, "But is it not dreadful that he should, with all his misfortunes on his mind, and perhaps wrought up to their climax, end his life without one jot of human happiness."

Though it was not original with him, Keats had chosen an effective phrase to make his point (there exist at least a half-dozen literary sources for it, including the *Philaster* of Beaumont and Fletcher, a copy of which he had with him). More interesting than the question of sources is the possibility that Keats in preferring an anonymous epitaph was not primarily expressing disgust or despair but was subtly assuring himself the ear of posterity. Not at all naive in such things, he certainly would have appreciated the curious appeal those few bare words would exert when encountered among all the named graves in a cemetery. He would have been well aware what a memorable impression they make. Mixed in the line, no doubt, was a degree of resentment at his fate, but surely Keats could not have missed its other, more positive impact.

Sinking steadily as the days passed—his face losing flesh so that now for the first time he appeared gaunt, with hollow, staring eyes, sharpened nose, and ashen cheeks—he roused one night to what can be seen as a final pathetic stab of poetic insight. Waking from a restless sleep, he saw Severn nodding in a chair by the bed. On a table a single candle, burning low, had begun to gutter. Reluctant to disturb Severn to ask for another, he watched as the light flickered and dimmed, when suddenly a tiny flame passed from the guttering candle through the darkness to a second candle whose wick on the instant blazed up. "Severn, Severn!" called Keats excitedly, "here's a little fairy lamplighter has actually lit up the other candle!"

Awake, the smiling Severn explained that, fearful he might fall asleep and not wanting Keats to open his eyes in a darkened room, he had tied a bit of string between the two candles. He was pleased that the experiment had worked so well.

In London by mid-February two more of Severn's letters had been received and duly circulated, those to Haslam of January 15th and to Taylor of January 25th–26th. The first, abruptly ending all hope for the recovery so bravely mentioned by Severn in his letter to Mrs. Brawne, informed everyone that consumption had at last been definitely identified. Keats' death, said the letter baldly, was now inevitable. The letter that followed enforced the bad news, saying that there was "less and less hope . . . the Doctor has most certainly done all that could be done, but he says that Keats should never have left England—the disease had made too great a progress . . . Nature can't hold out another fortnight."

The second letter arrived in London on February 17th, ten days beyond the fortnight specified, which meant that Keats might already be dead. Recognizing the possibility, all waited nervously for Severn's next communication. Meantime, the two January letters were withheld from Fanny: she was told that while Keats was no worse, neither was he any better. For her, the waiting and the daily apprehension almost turned fear into reality, and to Keats' sister she wrote, "All I do is persuade myself I shall never see him again." Brown, encountering Fanny often at Wentworth Place, was careful to drop no hint that all hope of recovery had fled. "She looks more sad every day," he reported.

Through the remainder of February no further word came from Rome. Then on March 5th Severn's long letter to Brown, written in mid-February, arrived with the news that Keats was still alive. Though much worse and still suffering, he had now become "reconciled to his horrible misfortune." Again Severn lamented the fact that they had ever left London, where Keats' death "might have been eased by the presence of his many friends."

That letter, at her mother's direction, was also withheld from Fanny, a course with which Brown disagreed. Keeping the worried girl in ignorance of the truth, he said, only caused her to imagine the worst, and he was sure that her resulting behavior proved him right. She was now acting very strangely, her moods swinging from one extreme to the other. At times her old habit of scintillating in company returned and she seemed in Brown's eyes nothing less than "boisterous." A string of glib remarks and comments came from her which were intended to be amusing but which "make one start rather than laugh." Then, grown suddenly quiet, she appeared to be brooding heavily and seemed "sinking under apprehension."

On March 9th Brown visited next door to say he was just then writing to Rome and would be glad to include some news of the Brawnes. Fanny and her mother were both in the room, and again Brown was puzzled by the younger woman's reaction, though refraining from any comment: "Miss Brawne said not a word and looked so incapable of speaking that I regretted having mentioned my writing to you before her."

By the time of that curious incident, Keats had been dead exactly fourteen days.

~

It was rather a startling request, making Severn feel decidedly uncomfortable, yet there was no way he could refuse. If Keats wanted him to go out and make a personal tour of the cemetery, bringing back a detailed description of the gravesite and its surroundings, he'd have to do it.

There was no difficulty about which cemetery it would be: the Protestant burial ground in the countryside on Rome's sprawling northern edge. Nor would the place be hard to find, situated as it was in the shadow of an old Roman monument, the lofty pyramidal tomb of the otherwise unknown Caius Cestius. Sometime in the three days, February 16–18, while the English nurse looked after the patient, Severn set out.

An open field it proved to be, hardly more than a tree-dotted meadow, set against the outside face of the old Roman wall. The gravestones, none large, stood in random clusters among the trees, fewer in number than Severn expected, only about fifty, with many of the mounds unmarked. Here and there stood some slightly more imposing monument, "surmounted by an urn of classical form and elegant design," showing by the "glittering whiteness of the marble that it was fresh from the hand of the sculptor." A profusion of wild-flowers, mostly violets and daisies, straying colorfully through the uncut grass "absolutely starred the turf." New graves, Severn found on inquiry, would be dug to one side of the cemetery. Keats' grave would be almost at the corner of the Cestius pyramid, where as part of the old Roman wall rose a mouldering, battlemented tower.

Strolling the grounds, wondering how best to describe for a dying man the spot of earth in which he'd be buried, Severn was pleased to encounter a sight he was sure would have a special appeal for Keats: browsing contentedly on the grass was a small flock of sheep with a few goats mixed in, tended by a young shepherd. Altogether, decided Severn happily, it was quite a lovely spot, serene in its pastoral isolation, comforting in its antiquated atmosphere, just the place for a vexed spirit to find rest.

Back at No. 26, stumbling a bit as he talked, Severn told the sick man of what he'd seen, giving it in as much detail as he could recall. Very gladly he heard Keats expressing much "pleasure at my descrip-tion of the locality," particularly the old tower and the riot of wild-flowers. Violets, said Keats, had always been his favorite, and now "he joyed to hear how they overspread the grave." However, Severn's relief at having so well executed the difficult assignment in the next moment was dashed a little as he heard Keats plaintively murmur that he could "feel the flowers growing over him."

Aside from the English nurse and occasionally the sculptor, young Ewing, no visitors now entered the apartment. When Ewing did show up he never stayed long, though always offering to take care of any shopping needed or other errands. Once he brought with him a stranger, a young Spaniard with literary ambitions, who'd heard the affecting tale of the dying English poet. The visit of the two took place about February 19th, but when they found how serious Keats' condition had become they soon left so as not to be in the way. They were the last outsiders to see the poet alive. (Nothing else is known of this visit, but the young Spaniard, Valentin Llanos, soon afterward went to London where he became a familiar in the Keats circle. In 1826 he married Keats' sister.)

Milk and a little bread were now almost Keats' only food, taken three or four times a day, the only sort of nourishment he could be sure of keeping down. By mid-February, inadequate diet combined with the effects of the illness produced a rapid weight loss, drastically altering his appearance. By the nineteenth in the eyes of the watching Severn the face of Keats had become "most ghastly," and that night for the first time he felt sure that death was imminent, a matter of hours at most. Standing or sitting by the bed through the long night, enduring the awful moans and the coughing so violent it seemed Keats must suffocate, he found himself wishing fervently that the release of death would come fast for his friend. Time after time he responded to Keats' helpless request that he be lifted to a sitting position to ease the cough and help loosen the stubborn phlegm. Slipping his arm under the thin shoulders, Severn would raise them, holding the wasted body upright until Keats asked to be lowered to the pillow again.

"Did you ever see anyone die?" Keats asked wanly during a quiet moment. Severn mumbled a no. "Well, then I pity you, poor Severn," Keats went on. "What trouble and danger you have got into for me. I

don't think I'll be convulsed, but be firm, for it won't last long. I shall
soon be laid in the quiet grave. Thank God for the quiet grave—O! I
can feel the cold earth upon me!" The cough ceasing that night, he
fell into a heavy sleep that lasted till dawn. Opening his bleared eyes
to the daylight next morning, realizing that he was still alive, he cried
out in frustration at having to face another day. "O how bitterly he
grieved" to find himself alive, recalled Severn.

   At intervals during the past weeks Severn had been adding to the
long letter he'd started for his family. On the morning of the twentieth, emotionally and physically drained by the previous night's
ordeal, he again took up the letter, penning another lengthy passage. In it Keats gets only a hurried mention, which may seem
strange ("Poor Keats cannot last but a few days more. I am now
quite reconciled to his state, yet I fear I shall feel the miss of him").
But Severn had not turned to his family letter to supply information on the poet's fate. He did so in a determined effort to forget,
for at least a little while, the awful looming of death. Sorely tried in
ways never anticipated, his youthful spirit was seeking in the solace
of family warmth a refuge from one of life's starkest moments.

   He opens by picturing himself back home once more, in his imagination having one of his hearty old talks with his favorite sister:

   My good-natured fire says good morning Maria, so while my
   kettle is boiling I will give you a little more gossip. Now sit down
   and make yourself comfortable. How do you do this morning?
   How are they all at home? How is Mother? Come now sit down
   and hear what I have got to say. Pull off your bonnet. You know
   you don't see me often. It must be now 5 months, a good long
   time. What a many changes I have seen . . .

Line after line he goes on, lightheartedly telling about his ocean voyage to Italy, about life in Naples, about his artistic concerns, about
everything and anything but life at No. 26. He ends with a request for
a long letter in return: "When you write don't apologize about it. I
shall always be delighted with your good scrawl."

It is well for Severn that he was able for those few moments over his breakfast on the morning of the twentieth to forget his weariness and the ugly scenes he'd endured. Again that night the ordeal began, again lasting through the night until dawn, and with the same result, Keats still reluctantly alive while wishing with all his heart for death. The night after that, the twenty-first, brought exactly the same: the moaning, the abandoned cries, the repeated sitting up in bed to lessen the tightening effect of the jarring cough, the drenching sweat covering the fevered body.

On the morning of the twenty-second, even worn out as he was by five consecutive nights without sleep, Severn managed to write another letter, a short note to his friend Haslam. In reality it is not so much a letter as it is a convulsive reaching out to touch the hand of sympathy:

> O! how anxious I am to hear from you—none of yours has come, but in answer to mine from Naples—I have nothing to break this dreadful solitude but letters—day after day—night after night—here I am by our poor dying friend—my spirit—my intellect and my health are breaking down—I can get no one to change me—no one will relieve me—they all run away—and even if they did not, poor Keats could not do without me . . .
>
> Last night I thought he was going—I could hear the phlegm in his throat—he bade me lift him up in bed or he would die with pain—I watched him all night—at every cough I expected he would suffocate—death is very fast approaching, for this morning by the pale daylight the change in him frightened me . . .

With that, carried along by the intensity of his feelings, unconsciously with a few bold strokes he sketches one of the truly poignant scenes in literary history:

> Poor Keats keeps me by him—and shadows out the form of one solitary friend—he opens his eyes in great horror and doubt—but when they fall upon me they close gently, and open

and close until he falls into another sleep—The very thought of this keeps me by him until he dies.

To this point in his letter, Severn had filled two large pages with his usual neat hand, the lines straight and evenly spaced. Near the bottom of page two the words and lines begin to sprawl, and when he reaches the top of the third page, the loss of control illustrates what he says: "I wont try to write any more—the want of sleep has almost taken away the power—the Post is going so I would try—think of me my dear Haslam as doing well and happy—as far as—will allow."

That night, the twenty-second, saw Severn again pass the interminable candlelit hours at Keats' bedside. Once more the two men together grimly greeted the dawn, Keats once more bemoaning his survival.

The English nurse, at first able to come only for some hours every other day, with Keats worsening had begun more frequent visits, each time staying longer. The aim was to permit Severn to catch an hour or two of uninterrupted sleep in the mornings. But even when he stretched out on the sofa in the sitting room, shutting his eyes and thinking only of oblivion, it didn't work. He couldn't get to sleep but lay there with his mind growing steadily duller and more numb. About mid-afternoon of the twenty-third the nurse as usual said goodbye and left. Pushing himself up off the sofa, Severn once more went doggedly into Keats' bedroom.

This day the racking cough began early, soon after four o'clock. His breath coming heavily as it required greater and greater effort to draw, Keats asked to be raised up. Under the yielding shoulders went Severn's right arm, feeling the nightclothes wringing with sweat, and he carefully pulled the emaciated body higher on the pillows. With each heave of the chest the phlegm could be heard boiling in his throat. His eyes, always large and luminous, now in the pale, shrunken face were enormous, their accustomed brightness "extreme." To Severn's spellbound stare the whole effect was "not earthly."

"Don't breathe on me," said Keats huskily, his face flushed and shining with moisture, "it comes like ice."

Through the rest of the afternoon and evening Keats several times asked to be lifted up or lowered. As darkness came on, his breathing grew more difficult, the rasp of the phlegm markedly increasing. Shortly after eleven P.M., lying at full length but still wide awake, he signaled that he wanted to be raised.

Severn's right arm again grasped the shoulders. As Keats sat up, he clutched at Severn's left hand, grasping it hard. The drawn expression on his face showed "extreme sensibility," but strangely no pain.

"Don't be frightened," said Keats after a while, his voice weak but calm as he repeated words he'd already used once or twice. "I'll die easy. Thank God it has come."

The labored rise and fall of the chest continued, but soon the rattling of phlegm slowly eased and grew quiet. Then the heavy breathing eased a bit. Sleep at last, blessed sleep, thought Severn, keeping his arm steady around the damp shoulders to avoid jostling. A few soundless minutes later, glancing down at the moistly glistening cheeks and eyelids, aware suddenly of how still, how ponderous seemed the weight in his arms, Severn realized that his friend was no longer breathing.

Gently he lowered the limp shoulders to the bed, the head settling onto the piled-up pillows. Gazing down at the lifeless figure, for many minutes Severn stood motionless, immense relief mixed with his sadness. "I confess that his pallid dead face was for a while to me a consolation," he later recalled, "for I had seen it express such suffering."

No mention of it comes from Severn. No surviving document refers to it. But one final circumstance of that mournful night may with confidence be pictured. As the labored breathing ceased, from the loosening grasp of the lifeless hand lying on the bed there rolled the reddish-white carnelian.

❧

For the exhausted Severn, emotionally and mentally wrung-out as he was, the week following Keats' death became something of a blur.

Fortunately, the good Dr. Clark took charge, making the necessary reports and arrangements. The body was removed to the morgue, and the apartment was sealed by the police, awaiting inspection by the health authorities. Severn was taken across the piazza to Clark's house where he found himself utterly unable to sleep but was made to rest. At the morgue the required autopsy was performed, confirming tuberculosis as the cause of death: "the lungs were completely gone—the doctors could not conceive how he had lived in the last 2 months." At the same time a death-mask was made, probably at Severn's insistence, and casts taken of the hand and foot.

Early on the morning of Monday, February 26th, as the coffin was about to be closed, Severn with his own hands placed Fanny's two unread letters, in protective wrapping along with a lock of her hair, inside the dead man's jacket, on the chest over the heart. Elsewhere in the coffin he put two letters from the poet's sister, and a little purse she'd made for him as a parting gift.

With Severn, Dr. Clark, William Ewing, and two or three other mourners, the slow-moving carriages of the funeral cortege wound through the streets and out into the countryside to the Protestant Cemetery. With the little group standing around the coffin in the shadow of the Cestius pyramid and the old Roman tower, the service was read by the Reverend Mr. Wolff, the English chaplain at Rome. By nine o'clock the coffin had been lowered, and the mourners were turning back to their carriages, when Dr. Clark stopped long enough to give some directions to the diggers. After closing the grave they were to bring sods of growing daisies and plant them, enough to cover the entire plot.

Next morning, remembering all those waiting anxiously in London, Severn forced himself to take up a pen and write a short note, addressed to Brown, who would spread the news:

He is gone—he died with the most perfect ease—he seemed to go to sleep—On the 23rd Friday at [1/2] past 4 the approaches of death came on . . . this increased until eleven at night when he gradually sank into death—so quiet that I still thought he slept . . .

It was Brown who told Fanny the news, carrying Severn's letter next door. He supplied no details of the meeting, however, so the scene cannot be reconstructed even in its outlines. But what he did say, though it impinges on a difficult moment for the young woman, may not be passed over too quickly.

No doubt her mother was present. Brown was aware that the girl had been spared the accumulating bad news of the previous weeks, thus she could legitimately be expecting her fiancé to survive many months at least. In that case he would have been especially diffident and wary in approaching his delicate task. He would have found he needn't have worried.

The initial jolt to the girl was indeed severe, says Brown, an unavoidable result, and perhaps largely because of the surprise. Yet her recovery was rapid, and her behavior thereafter was curiously controlled, so much so that Brown remarked on it. "It is now five days since she heard it," he wrote to Severn. "I shall not speak of the first shock, nor of the following days—it is enough she is now pretty well—and thro'out she has shown a firmness of mind which I little expected from one so young, and under such a load of grief."

During those five days Brown encountered her frequently ("thro'out," he says). Each time, it is clear, he was much impressed by her mental balance in the face of her terrible loss, her ability, despite her youth, to hold sudden, wrenching grief at arm's length.

SEVEN

GLOWING PROSPECTS

In a small apartment at No. 18 via di San Isidoro, a five-minute walk from the Piazza di Spagna, Joseph Severn tried to settle himself down to the task of completing his Academy painting, much behind schedule. It was now a real question whether he could hope to complete it in time to be shipped to London for the judging. Even so, he found it a struggle to wield a brush, for still horribly vivid in his memory was the wrenching experience of his friend's cruel death.

In addition, the authorities were insisting on payment for the infected furniture, all now destroyed—sent up in flames in a huge pile in the middle of the piazza—and for the cleaning and overhauling of the death chamber. Two weeks after the funeral he was still in a state of nervous debility and apologizing to his friend Taylor in London for his silence:

"I have tried many times to write to you—but no—I could not it has been too much for me to think on it—I have been ill from the fatigue and pain I have suffered—the recollection of poor Keats hangs dreadfully upon me—I see him at every glance . . . These brutal Italians have nearly finished their monstrous business—they have burned all the furniture and are now scraping the walls—making new windows—new doors—and even a new floor." It was a natural reaction, even inevitable, to the termination of his lengthy ordeal, and those early March days represented perhaps the lowest point in Severn's young life.

Then, suddenly, in mid-March, in the deepest stage of his heavy depression, everything changed. As the story of the young painter's heroic tending of the dying poet went the rounds of Rome's large English colony, filtering back to England as well, distinguished visitors began calling at the Isidoro street apartment, leaving the lonely Severn feeling "astonished." Knocking at his door, apologetically introducing themselves, were artists of all sorts, members of the aristocracy, noble lords and ladies, and the simply affluent. All wished to meet Severn, to thank him for doing what he did, to compliment his unselfishness and his largeness of heart. More to the point, almost without exception they offered encouragement and help in his chosen career.

An abundance of painting suplies of every kind was showered on him, and he was also provided with a piano. He was invited out for dinners and parties at palaces and country villas. He was given the use of a sumptuous studio, the property of the eminent English artist Charles Eastlake, then absent from the city. Through April the parade of well-wishers continued, and by May Severn had recovered from his downcast state sufficiently to realize and fully appreciate what was happening to him. This was not, he saw, a mere passing fad of the rich. A chord had been touched, reaching something fundamental in the deepest, most sensitive part of human aspiration—and at last Severn knew it.

Early in May he wrote Haslam in London saying he'd found many new friends, "but you can't imagine to what extent." He explains all about his good fortune (only the night before, he says proudly, he dined at the table of Lord Colchester, sitting between Baron Ruthven and Lady Westmoreland), which now included many commissions for paintings. "This place is everything for me." he explains happily, "I look forward with great hope and delight—I have the most glowing prospect before me—a noble profession—a prospect of capital health in the finest situation in the World—I have youth and above all I have a very contented mind—anything satisfies me—I can live on very little—so, my dear fellow, it will be a long time before you see me back." For Haslam's part in persuading him to leave England and come to Rome as Keats' companion, he adds fervently, "Thanks thanks—to the end of my days."

In July he finished his Academy painting, *The Death of Alcibiades*, and sent it up to London. Though tardy in arriving, it was promptly awarded the coveted fellowship, setting him financially at ease for at least three full years. A benefit of a different kind reached him in December when he was paid a fine tribute by Shelley, a tribute which was to make his name a permanent part of English literature. The poem, *Adonais*, Shelley's magnificent elegy on the death of Keats, carried a short introduction which concluded with a mention of the fact that the dying poet had been accompanied to Italy,

> by Mr. Severn, a young artist of the highest promise, who, I have been informed, "almost risked his own life, and sacrificed every prospect to unwearied attendance upon his dying friend." Had I known these circumstances before the completion of my poem, I should have been tempted to add my feeble tribute of applause to the more solid recompense which the virtuous man finds in the recollection of his own motives.
>
> Mr. Severn can dispense with a reward from "such stuff as dreams are made of." His conduct is a golden augury of the success of his future career: may the unextinguished spirit of his illustrious friend animate the creations of his pencil, and plead against Oblivion for his name!

Reading those enthusiastic words at that particular time brought tears of joy and gratitude to Severn's eyes. As a source of inspiration in his art, the concluding phrase of Shelley's statement following the the colon he copied in large letters and hung on the wall of his studio.

He continued to live and work in Rome, now and then traveling round the country to fulfill painting commissions. At last in 1828 he found a wife, the beautiful niece of Lady Westmoreland. Married and enjoying Rome more than ever, he passed another decade in busy contentment before he again thought of returning to England to live. By the time he departed in the summer of 1841, he was the father of five children (a sixth would be born in London), and had an enviable reputation as a painter with a name almost as well known as that of the poet himself.

※

The question of an epitaph for Keats' gravestone was not easily settled. As those concerned saw the matter, there were some problems about using only the one bitter line Keats had dictated to Severn. The form of the stone also caused uncertainty as well as the question of who among the several sculptors in Rome who'd volunteered should execute it. At last John Gibson was chosen and the design settled on, an idea of Severn's: at the top of the stone, above the inscription, would appear a Greek lyre showing half the strings broken. This would signify both Keats' classical genius and the great promise cut short by his early death.

Earnest discussion about the inscription went on for almost two years, shuttling back and forth in the post between Rome and London, with Brown, Haslam, Hunt, Taylor, and Severn all having a say. What would be the effect if the stone carried only those bare words specified by the poet? Wasn't something more needed by way of explanation? Taylor felt that nothing could be better than Keats' own "melancholy comment," standing unaccompanied, without a name or even a date. Just that one short, challenging line, said Taylor, would soon become "as clear an indication to posterity as the plainest, everyday inscription that one may find in Westminster Abbey."

Brown disagreed. A gravestone epitaph, he insisted, is most often read as if composed by the friends of the deceased, not as if the deceased himself had written it. Some brief explanation must be included to show clearly that the line did not come from grieving friends but from the dead man. Taken as the sentiment of the survivors, Keats words simply weren't fitting. Perhaps something like this, Brown suggested, going to the opposite extreme: "This grave contains all that was mortal of a young English poet who, on his death-bed, in bitter anguish at the neglect of his countrymen, desired these words to be engraven on his tombstone: HERE LIES ONE WHOSE NAME WAS WRIT IN WATER." That wasn't quite right, either, Brown cautioned, but it gave a start. Then quickly he added that if the others agreed with Taylor's approach he was quite ready, despite his strong feelings, to give way.

In such a desultory manner was Keats' dramatic farewell to the world defeated. Severn, left to decide on his own, perhaps grown tired of the long-distance debate, unfortunately made the wrong choice. Siding with Brown but ignoring the caution, and giving no thought to the obvious honing required in Brown's text, he wrote back that "It shall be done" exactly as it stood in the letter.* Late in 1822 Gibson finished his part of the task, and Severn set the stonecutter to work chipping the epitaph into the gray surface just as Brown had written it. The "sad office" of supervising erection of the stone at the grave was performed by Severn in February 1823: "I shall put some Evergreens around it of course."

Before many years had passed, when all concerned had gained some emotional distance from the affecting moment, it was agreed that Keats' own few words, unadorned, would have been infinitely better.

---

*He did make one change, hardly an improvement, and further misplacing the emphasis. He deleted the words, "in bitter anguish at the neglect of his countrymen," putting in their place, "in the bitterness of his heart at the malicious power of his enemies." But the phrase dictated by Keats was a cry not against any supposed "enemies," but against the unkind fate that had robbed him, as he thought, of his full share of life and fame.

EIGHT

THE GIRL HE LEFT BEHIND

In a small, neat house near Eaton Square in London, one of a long row of identical dwellings along Coleshill Street, lived Mr. Louis Lindon and his wife, the former Fanny Brawne. Still with them were two of their three children, a son Herbert, aged twenty-seven, and a daughter Margaret, aged twenty-one. Edmund, the oldest at thirty-one, was on his own in foreign service. Far from affluent, the family still managed to live comfortably on Mr. Lindon's salary as a sales agent. His wife's considerable inheritance, which in earlier days had made such a difference, had at last dried up.

Now in her sixty-fifth year, Mrs. Lindon was not at all well, being troubled by a dangerous combination of asthma and angina. It was that disturbing fact, her questionable health, that led to a curious and fateful incident in the Lindon home in the fall of 1865. Of that event no precise record has survived, yet its outlines can with some assurance be recovered from the surrounding evidence. Equally certain, on that same evidence, is the fact that the incident took place only after Mr. Lindon was safely out of the house for the day.

By now a semi-invalid, spending part of her time resting in bed or on a sofa, one day in October or November 1865, Fanny called Herbert and Margaret to her room. As the two listened raptly, their fascination growing by the minute, she proceeded to unfold a strange tale out of her past. It was a story her children had never heard before, never even suspected, telling of her youthful love for an obscure young poet, long since dead. As she talked she opened a small box, laying out its contents on a table. Among the items were some half-dozen books, a lock of reddish hair in a gold case, a miniature of a young man with reddish hair, a ring set with a purplish-red almandine, and several batches of old letters.

These things, said Fanny, were all she had left of her girlish romance. The young poet she identified as the unfortunate John Keats, who had died so young and in such obscurity, but who since had become so famous.

The books on the table included Keats' own three volumes of poetry, as well as the works of Dante, Shakespeare, Spenser, and Milton—each volume showing many marginal notations in Keats' firm hand. The lock of reddish hair was also his, given to Fanny as he departed on his final journey. The letters, several dozen of them, had been written to their mother, each fervently declaring his consuming love for her. The ring was one he'd given her at their engagement in the fall of 1819.

She was telling her children all this, explained Fanny, because she feared that her end was near. Their father's absence from the room was necessary because he knew nothing of the old affair, nor was he *ever* to know—that was her firm stipulation. During more than thirty years of marriage she had kept her secret from her husband, never allowing him to see or even know of the contents of the little box. He was aware that his wife had been acquainted with the young poet, knew that Keats, as many another young man, had "admired" her. But that was all. Because Fanny wished to have it so, even after all those years together her husband still had, as she put it, "a very imperfect idea" of the truth. Whether she went on, that day, to explain her reason for the secrecy, is the one major element which cannot be teased from the evidence. Even if the children inquired about it, which no doubt they did, it seems that no clear answer was given, at least no inkling of one survives.

Now it was the turn of her children, said Fanny, to safeguard the relics she had kept for half a century. They must preserve their mother's secret until their father too had passed on. Afterward, they might do as they wished with the things in the box, always remembering that the relics, the letters especially, would—this is the exact phrase quoted by Herbert from his mother—"someday be considered of value." Exactly what sort of value was meant, whether literary or monetary, was never made explicit. It can only be said that, thereafter, Fanny's son, with ample opportunity to alter the perception, permitted the latter meaning to stand.

One further thought was presented to her children by Fanny that day, the idea that the thirty-nine letters written to her by Keats comprised an important part of his biography. For long she had felt that—intimately and even starkly revealing of the poet as they were—at some time they would be published—and *should*, she added.

Thrilled, and no little astonished, to hear such revelations about their mother, the two Lindons had no difficulty in discovering more about that early love. During the intervening decades the obscure young poet had indeed gained a high and ever-growing reputation. The existence of such a romantic entanglement was by then an established part of the record, always with the woman's identity shielded. Nearly fifty years after Keats' death, the name of the woman he'd loved so passionately was still unknown to the public. It lived only in the aging memories of a few old friends and acquaintances.

First to mention the old affair, of course leaving out the lady's name, had been Leigh Hunt in his widely circulated sensationalist memoir of 1828, *Lord Byron and Some of His Contemporaries*. Poor Keats' many hardships over his health and poetic career, wrote Hunt, had been "secretly" aggravated by a very tender circumstance "which I can but allude to thus publically." The affair, he said, had imposed a great deal of emotional turmoil on "one of the warmest hearts and imaginations that ever existed." Once a despondent Keats "with tears in his eyes," had confessed to him that because of some unspecified upheaval in his romance "his heart was breaking." Hunt knew the lady's name, knew much of the true story. Only his feeling for his old friend, and the custom of the time, held him back.

Twenty years after Hunt, the Lindons found, more about the affair became available, presented in the pages of the pioneer biography published in 1848, *The Life and Letters of John Keats*, by R. M. Milnes. Reading what Milnes wrote about their mother, still in carefully veiled fashion, Herbert and Margaret must have blinked in disbelief: was this the proper, practical self-controlled woman they'd known and loved since childhood!

Telling how love had dawned for the poet, Milnes used strong language. From the outset of his chronicle he actually presents the affair as a contributing factor, in fact a leading element in Keats' early death. "The time was at hand," wrote Milnes, "when one intense affection was about to absorb his entire being, and to hasten, by its very violence, the calamitous extinction against which it struggled in vain." The lady in question had exerted on the susceptible poet no small or transient power, inspiring him with "a passion that only ceased with his existence."

To identify the lady, Milnes went on, or to dwell too closely on details, would at that time be not only "indecorous" but decidedly "intrusive." Yet with that he hardly pauses in his narrative, hurrying on to explain that a marriage between the poet and the mysterious young woman had been prevented only by strained finances, "plain poverty," later made worse by deteriorating health, "mortal sickness." With that the biographer gave way more recklessly still, hinting that the woman in question was even then alive.

The overpowering effect of such an intense and demanding love on the poet, stated Milnes, had had its undesirable, its downright bad side. It had

> conquered the physical man, and made the very intensity of his passion, in a certain sense, accessory to his death: he might have lived longer if he had lived less [Milnes may have intended to write "loved less," which better fits the context]. But this should be no matter of self-reproach to the object of his love, for the same may

be said of his poetic faculty, and of all that made him what he was. It is enough that she has preserved his memory with a sacred honour, and it is no vain assumption that to have inspired and sustained the one passion of this noble being has been a source of grave delight and earnest thankfulness, through the changes and chances of her earthly pilgrimage.

First had come Hunt with his talk of the emotional strain caused by the affair, then came Milnes with his strange if shadowy picture of the "violence" of affection which had hastened Keats' demise—his passion becoming "accessory" to his early death. To Herbert and his sister, to say the least, it must have appeared that their mother's youthful romance had been far from an unbroken idyll.

Also available in the 1848 biography was Keats' own testimony, at least partially supporting Milnes' graphic portrait. In separate letters, both written to Charles Brown, the Lindons could read of the poet's sadly wrenching fear and sorrow as his enforced parting from their mother approached. "The thought of leaving Miss ——— is beyond everything horrible," he confesses in the first letter, "—the sense of darkness coming over me—I eternally see her figure eternally vanishing." In the second letter he bursts out with a similar anguished cry: "I cannot bear to leave her. O, God! God! God! Everything I have in my trunk that reminds me of her goes through me like a spear . . . my imagination is horribly vivid about her—I see her—I hear her . . . O, that I could be buried near where she lives!" Even to be reminded of her is torture, he says, and adds that the sight of her handwriting on a letter would break his heart. "Where can I look for consolation . . . If I had any chance of recovery, this passion would kill me."

Milnes also, the two found, gave one of the many love poems that Keats had written to their mother (titling it only "To ———," but stating quite clearly that it had been written to the loved Miss ———). In several of the lines Herbert and Margaret were able to glimpse their mother in willing response to her insistent young lover. "Touch has a memory," Keats wrote pointedly, and he illustrates his meaning by recalling the way his "aching arms" had clasped the slender waist, how the willing girl's "warm breath" had made a stirring in his hair. "Give me those lips again!" he cries in one line, and in another begs to be allowed to rest once more on "that dazzling breast!"

A third source, more recent, while being careful to veil the girl's name as well as the turmoil of the affair, would have ratified for the Lindon offspring what they'd found in Hunt and Milnes. It was an article in the *Atlantic Monthly* for April 1863, written by Joseph Severn himself, the only article on Keats he ever published. For Severn now, speaking to the public, all the old original doubts and uncertainties, expressed by so many regarding the affair, had evaporated:

> For more than the year I am now dwelling on, he had fostered a tender and enduring love for a young girl nearly his own age, and this was reciprocal, not only in itself, but in all the worldly advantages arising from it of fortune on her part and fame on his. It was encouraged by the sole parent of the lady; and the fond mother was happy in seeing her daughter so betrothed, and pleased that her inheritance would fall to so worthy an object as Keats. This was all well settled in the minds and hearts of the mutual friends of both parties . . .

Having learned of this remarkable new dimension in the early life of their staid and now seriously ailing parent, the Lindon offspring had little time to seek for details. By late November 1865 Fanny's condition had worsened, and shortly afterward she died. No further information on that event is to be had, nothing of her last days or hours, of her funeral or her will, or the disposition of her effects. On December 8th, the *Times* in its crowded obituary column on the front page included her name among more than thirty others: "On the 4th inst., at 34, Coleshill-street, Eaton-square, Frances, the wife of Louis Lindon, Esq. Friends will kindly accept this intimation." By then the Lindons' friends could not have been plentiful, and in any

case most still lived on the continent. None left on record any reference to her passing, at least no record remains.

Her husband, as it developed, survived her less than seven years,
dying in October 1872, cause not known.

It was then, most probably, that his son and daughter, as they
arranged the funeral things and looked after their father's papers,
made the interesting discovery that the difference in age between
their parents had been a full twelve years. In some surprise they also
found that it was their mother who had been the older.

Far back in the summer of 1833, as Fanny and Louis stood at the
altar of St. Marylebone Parish Church in London exchanging vows,
she was within weeks of her thirty-third birthday. He was barely
twenty-one.

⁂

Fanny's own keen awareness that she had been the chosen one, confidently declared Milnes, the woman destined to inspire the love of the
noble Keats, must ever after have given her abundant reason for
"grave delight." She in her turn, added the biographer, having "preserved his memory with a sacred honour," richly deserved to be com-
mended. In expressing such sentiments, apparently, Milnes was
being no more than just and of course quite sincere—his own
integrity is not in question. But if so, it can only mean that he never
saw a certain letter written by Fanny twenty years before, long prior
to the start of his work on the biography. Had Milnes seen that letter
he would assuredly have paused long before writing what he did
about Fanny and her sacred trust.

At first, it seems true, she did feel the heavy burden of her lost
love, as is indicated by what she wrote Keats' sister long before, some
three months after his death. While his friends by then had gotten
past the initial shock, she declares emphatically, "I have not got over
it and never shall." Grimly committed at that time to Keats' memory,
she felt unable even to speak with anyone who failed to mourn suffi-

ciently, people "too uninterested in him to have any right to mention what is to you and me so great a loss." Her sorrowing words at this time, it may be agreed, do carry an authentic ring of dedication. Yet only a few years were required to bring a drastic dilution of that reverential mood.

By December 1829 Fanny can be heard blithely announcing herself to be entirely "unconnected" with the dead poet, at the same time saying she wished he could be forgotten by the public. Less than ten years after Keats' death, a very different Fanny Brawne felt only "the odium" of being intimately linked with someone who had been so out of favor with fate. Fanny's 1829 letter was not recently discovered. For almost fifty years it has been readily accessible to anyone interested. But fitting it into the puzzle of Fanny's life has cost scholars and critics considerable hardship. The result has been a curious if tacit conspiracy of silence regarding the letter, at least its more troubling parts (the major Keats biographers, Ward, Bate, and Gittings, all chose virtually to ignore the letter, slipping past it tight-lipped).

Fanny's sole biographer, Joanna Richardson, in her very sympathetic treatment of her subject (a slim volume of some 150 text pages, much of it little more than conjecture), does quote the letter. But its most damning sentence she quietly drops out, transferring it to the relative obscurity of the book's notes. The letter as a whole she simply dismisses, on the ground that when writing it Fanny was suffering a "profound disturbance of her mind" over the recent accidental death of her mother. In bland contradiction of the obvious, she says that in the letter Fanny shows "an unselfish devotion" to Keats' fame while proclaiming her "supreme interest in his rightful reputation." On the contrary, Fanny's 1829 letter—what survives is actually a near-final draft—reveals a mind under perfect control as well as a heart feeling itself well rid of its youthful allegiance.

When the letter was written, Fanny, then twenty-nine, was still living at Wentworth Place and had not yet met her future husband. The interim period after Keats' death has left on record very little of a personal nature about her, but one revealing incident, accidentally preserved, shows that even while recovering from a recent illness she retained her scintillating bent. At a dinner party held at Wentworth Place earlier that year, one of the guests, a young literary hopeful named Gerald Griffin (later to gain notice as a novelist), found himself mightily impressed by his hostess. Writing to his sister some days later he says that Miss Brawne was "most animated—lively and even witty in conversation. She quite dazzled me in spite of her pale looks." Aware of Fanny's link with Keats, Griffin next gets off a fairly peculiar remark, which shows that he had noticed or heard something else about Fanny, something less than favorable. "If I were certain that the whole article were equal to the specimen given, how I should wish that my dear Lucy had such a friend and companion in her solitude! And how I should pity poor Keats!" What it was that sparked his doubts as to the *whole* woman—small enough, it may have been—Griffin fails to say.

The letter in question answered one from Charles Brown, then planning a biography of his friend, asking Fanny's agreement in using one of the Keats letters mentioning the love affair. "The question is will you object to it," inquired Brown deferentially. "Though much of it regards you, your name is never once mentioned . . . I shall of course scrupulously avoid intimating who you are, or in what part of England you reside." He also wanted to use some of the poetry Keats had addressed to her. "Think of it in your best train for thinking, my dear Miss Brawne, and let me know your decision."

It was a fairly lengthy reply that Fanny wrote to Brown.* She gives him the permission requested, but only after some curiously convoluted discussion, all of which shows her to be in full possession of herself, not at all "disturbed." Brown had mentioned the "long silence" between them (by then he'd been living in Florence for several years), a remark her opening acknowledges in her typical sprightly, almost teasing manner:

---

*For clarity, Fanny's run-on draft is here paragraphed, and a few capitals and periods inserted. The draft in its full original form may be consulted in the Forman edition of Keats' letters (1952), Vol. IV, lxii–lxiv.

Hampstead Decr 29th 1829

My dear Mr Brown

As the aggressor I am too happy to escape the apologies I owe you on my long silence not gladly to take your hint and say nothing about it. The best reparation I can make is to answer your letter of today as soon as possible although I received it only this morning.

In the hours that have intervened before I sat down to answer it my feelings have entirely changed on the subject of the request it contains. Perhaps you will think I was opposed to it and am now come over to your side of the question, but it is just the contrary. Had I answered your letter immediately I should have told you that I considered myself so entirely unconnected with Mr Keats except by my own feelings that nothing published respecting him could affect me. But now I see it differently.

We all have our little world in which we figure and I cannot help expressing some disinclination at the idea that the few acquaintances I have should be able to obtain such a key to my sensations. Having said so much you will probably conclude that I mean to refuse your request. Perhaps when I assure you that, though my opinion has changed, my intention of complying in every respect with your wishes remains, you will think I am mentioning my objections to make a favor of my consent. But indeed my dear Mr Brown if you do, you mistake me entirely. It is only to justify myself I own that I state all I think . . .

I assure you I should not have hinted that your wishes were painful to me did I not feel the suffering myself to be even alluded to was a want of pride. So far am I from possessing overstrained delicacy that the circumstance of its being a mere love story is the least of my concern. On the contrary, had I been his wife I should have felt my present reluctance would have been so much stronger that I think I must have made it my request that you would relinquish your intention. The only thing that saves me now is that so very few can know I am in any way implicated, and that of those few I may hope the greater number may never see the book in question.

Do then entirely as you please, and be assured that I comply with your wishes rather because they are yours than with the expectation of any good that can be done. I fear the kindest act would be to let him rest for ever in the obscurity to which unhappy circumstances have condemned him . . .

Such a painfully winding explanation carries its own interest, telling much about the writer herself, especially on such a topic. But at this point in her letter Fanny is only beginning to hit her stride. As she goes on, the meandering quality of her comment increases, now with an element of real uncertainty detectable. Will Keats' writings, she asks, be sufficient to rescue him from obscurity:

You can tell better than I, and are more impartial on the subject, for my wish has long been that his name, his very name, could be forgotten by everyone but myself. *That* I have often wished most intensely. I was more generous ten years ago. I should not now endure the odium of being connected with one who was working his way up against poverty and every sort of abuse.

To your publishing his poems addressed to me I do not see there can be any objection after the subject has once been alluded to, if you think them worthy of him. I entirely agree with you that if his life is to be published no part ought to be kept back, for all you can do is show his character. His life was too short and too unfortunate for anything else. I have no doubt that his talents would have been great . . . all I fear is whether he has left enough to make people believe that. If I could think so I should consider it right to make that sacrifice to his reputation that I do now to your kind motives.

Not that even the establishment of his fame would give me the pleasure it ought. Without claiming too much constancy for myself, I may truly say that he is well-remembered by me and that, satisfied with that, I could wish no one but myself knew he had ever existed . . .

She ends her letter with the most casually unsettling admission of all, openly doubting that Keats was really the man she once thought he was. Mentioning some negative critical comment recently written on the poet's supposed "weakness" of character, she states her own view:"I should be glad if you could disprove I was a very poor judge of character ten years ago and probably overrated every good quality he had, but surely they go too far on the other side." The tangled thought in those phrases, when unwound, becomes all too clear. Fanny is saying that, looking back, she finds her former high opinion of Keats as a man is no longer warranted: she had "overrated" him.

As to why she changed her mind, there exists no direct hint (though it at least deserves recording that in the meantime she had become a fairly wealthy woman, inheriting from her brother who died in 1828, and from her mother). There are only her remarks about being"more generous" ten years before, and about not liking to recall how she once gave her heart to a little-known young poet struggling to find his way.

꒰

After the affair of the Brown letter, a full dozen years flit by before Fanny again comes into view. Then a wife and mother, she can be heard or overheard, reluctantly explaining to her husband about her long-ago acquaintance with Mr. Keats but supplying no more information than she felt was needed or could get away with. That incident, in its turn, leads on to two others equally significant, one of them eight years further on, the other no less than twenty. Together the three events—interludes, they might be justly styled, or tableaux—lead the investigator on a giddy chase indeed, in its way only fitting where the delectable Fanny is concerned.

Following Fanny's wedding in June 1833 she and her husband left England to live in Germany, near Dusseldorf, where Lindon had both friends and family. Over the next few years the two moved about on the continent, mostly in Germany and France, returning to London for short visits. One such return took place in 1840, and involved a social call on Fanny's old friends, the Dilkes, then permanently settled in London. Whether Louis Lindon had by then heard the name of Keats in connection with that of his wife, cannot be said. But while at the Dilke home he noticed a portrait of the poet and inquired of his hostess who the young man might be. Unsure how much of the story Fanny had revealed to her husband, Mrs. Dilke delayed her reply. The unexpected reaction left Lindon in some puzzlement.

"To prevent awkward mistakes in future," Fanny declared to Mrs. Dilke afterward, "when we got home [I] explained as much as was necessary." Revealingly she added that had it not been for that one fleeting moment of hesitation over the picture, her unsuspecting husband "never would have heard of it." Even now, she goes on in curiously guarded fashion, he still had "a very imperfect idea of the real case. *Perhaps thinks his wife had an admirer, the more.*" (The italics are Fanny's, obviously meant to warn Mrs. Dilke how far she might go on the matter in talk.) What it was that might prove "awkward" if Lindon knew of his wife's girlish romance must be left open. At the moment no clue beckons.

The second of the three events began to take shape when the Lindons, in 1842, moved to Heidelberg, settling into an already sizable English colony. Also resident then was Thomas Medwin, at work on a biography of his cousin, Shelley. An inquisitive sort, Medwin was always, as Fanny said, "on the hunt for literary prey." In time the Lindons met him, liked him, and invited him several times to their home. There one day he came across what he saw as an unusual literary treasure, the volume of Shakespeare that had belonged to Keats, and which Medwin "by chance stumbled on." The phrase is Fanny's own, raising but not answering the question of how a guest might *stumble* on an item always stored safely away.

Anxious to include something of Keats in his biography of Shelley, Medwin kept at Fanny, asking for further information but without success. Only when another volume about Shelley reached her hands did she relent, the well-known *Essays, Letters From Abroad,* etc., edited by Mrs. Shelley and published in 1840. Reading the book Fanny was, as she says, "much shocked at a letter written by a Mr. Finch," which gave a very distorted account of "the last few weeks of poor Keats life." Hoping to counteract the wrong impression left by Finch, she supplied Medwin with certain original materials, including the letters written to her mother from Italy by Keats and Severn, and a copy of Severn's long letter to Brown sent just before Keats's death. In addition she wrote out a statement of her own which she allowed Medwin to use verbatim. When the Medwin volume appeared, in 1847, it had a short section on Keats with Fanny's materials prominent. Her name, again, was left unmentioned. The only reference made to a source identified an anonymous "lady who knew him well, better indeed than any individual out of his own family."

The Finch letter (he was a friend of Severn's in Rome, a wealthy English eccentric who styled himself Colonel Robert Finch) had been written in June 1821. It reported on Keats' last days using information received from Severn, but with a good deal of exaggeration. The few flashes of wrathful temper that arose in the dying Keats, Finch erected into a sustained crumbling of spirit: "He soon took to his bed from which he never rose more. His passions were always violent and his sensibility most keen. It is extraordinary that, proportionally as his strength of body declined, these acquired fresh vigour; and his temper at length became so outrageously violent as to injure himself, and annoy everyone around him." These passionate outbursts, said Finch, had been so extreme that the dying man "might be judged insane."

Fanny's statement in reply, as printed by Medwin, sincere and confidently outspoken as it is, actually becomes a significant if unwitting document in the story of her own love affair with the poet. Rather obviously, looking back through the misty decades, she has something more personal in mind than the annoying Colonel Finch. In reality she is remembering all the despairing anger that had been aimed at her in a stream of letters by the jealous Keats, anger she at last understands and excuses. Now in her fifties, ten years a wife, mother of two, she can better appreciate how her own unthinking behavior when young had generated his "savage despondency," as she here names it. The Finch letter, she says, is calculated to give

a very false idea of Keats. That his sensibility was most acute is true, and his passions were very strong, but not violent, if by that term violence of temper is implied. His [temper] was no doubt susceptible, but his anger seemed rather to turn on himself than on others, and in moments of greatest irritation it was only by a sort of savage despondency that he sometimes grieved and wounded his friends. Violence such as the letter describes was quite foreign to his nature.

For more than a twelvemonth before quitting England I saw him every day, often witnessed his sufferings, both mental and bodily, and I do not hesitate to say that he never could have addressed an unkind expression, much less a violent one, to any human being . . . Mr. Finch's letter goes on to say "Keats might be judged insane"—I believe the fever that consumed him might have brought on a temporary species of delirium, that made his friend Mr Severn's task a painful one.

It was a praiseworthy thing to do, speaking up for Keats in the face of her long-standing reticence. She must have known she was running a decided risk of exposure, that her name and present identity might easily be found out, by curious reviewers and journalists if no one else. Her husband, in fact, as a direct result of her Medwin involvement did make a momentary approach to her secret, only to be again steered away. Soon after publication of the Medwin volume he paid a visit to the home of another English resident at Heidelberg, Mrs. Caroline de Crespigny, and very soon found himself being questioned as to his wife's possible connection with Keats. Was Fanny the unidentified "lady" who supplied Medwin's information, Mrs. de Crespigny asked. But the evidence for the episode is so fleeting it will be best to give it in Fanny's own words. Talking of the fact that one of Keats' letters had been addressed not to herself but to Mrs. Brawne, she wonders whether it might "have seemed odd" to some readers for the older woman to have had "such and intimacy" with the youthful poet. She goes on:

> But cunning Mrs. de Crespigny was not to be taken in, & asked Mr. Lindon on his next visit, whether Mr. Keats had been an admirer of Mrs. Lindon's—and he, taken by surprise, knew just enough to answer yes.

There Fanny drops the subject, ignoring what must have been the episode's denouement. By all the rules of human nature, on reaching home that day from the de Crespigny house, Louis would have had another, closer look at the Medwin volume. Perhaps he would have paused especially over the claim that the lady and the poet had seen each other "every day" during his entire last year in England. With that, some curious discussion between husband and wife *must* have followed. Yet, as later events demonstrate, Fanny was again able to extricate herself, readily denying that she had filled the role of the "lady" who'd known the poet so well.

Why did Fanny say that she and Keats had seen each other every day in 1820 before he departed for Italy, when in reality they were apart a good deal of the time?

What did she tell Louis in July 1848 when the Milnes biography of Keats appeared, successfuly denying that she was the poet's "one intense affection," the woman who had so entrammeled and troubled him?

Not every question that can be asked about the elusive Fanny can be given an explicit answer. Or needs one.

Opening the little box on the table, Fanny Lindon, alone in the room, examined her Keats treasures carefully, dwelling on each of the half-dozen items separately. At last she made up her mind. If something had to be sold, it would be the miniature painting of the poet, an exquisite portrait from life done in oils on ivory. The letters she'd received from him almost a half-century ago—there were then more than forty in all—would bring a greater financial return, but she decided it was not yet time to make use of them. With the impact made by the Milnes biography, and with several editions of the poetry and one of the letters now available, Keats' place among the English poets was indeed established and steadily growing. The longer the love letters were held back the more valuable would they become. In any case, so long as Mr. Lindon was alive, while they might be sold in a strictly private way, they couldn't be published, lessening their potential value.

It was now the year 1860. The Lindons, after almost three decades of continental living, were back in England to stay. Whether they were already at the Coleshill Street house can't be said, but they were in London. They were also, it seems, in some sort of financial hardship, of an undetermined nature and extent. Apparently, Louis had lost his position as English sales agent for several foreign companies, and was now employed as a "wine merchant's clerk." With two sons in their twenties to be launched in life and a teenage daughter to be properly groomed, more money than ever was needed. The Keats miniature—it had been painted by Joseph Severn in 1818 and presented to Fanny on Keats' departure for Italy—would be a start. The difficulty was in deciding how best to go about it. What avenue for sale would bring the largest and readiest return?

An auction was too public. A professional dealer probably could find more confidential ways of locating a buyer, but even there, with the miniature out of her hands, she ran some risk of exposure. To be safe, it would have to pass directly from Fanny's own hand into the buyer's possession, someone who would agree to keep the purchase a secret. Luckily she knew just the man. Keats' old friend Charles Dilke had not only prospered in the world, as editor of the *Athenaeum* and by means of his own criticism, he had also become a power in literary circles. More to the point, he was an avid collector of Keats memorabilia.

The contact was made by letter, and a portion of that letter still exists, though in fragments. Its two remaining parts in their pregnant brevity are endlessly tantalizing, raising the interesting question of what was said in the parts thrown away. In the first fragment the unexpected offer is made:

"I am induced to ask whether it would suit you to purchase that minature of Mr. Keats which has been for so long a time in my possession. It would not be a light motive that would make me part with it, but I have this satisfaction, that next to my own family there is no one in whose possession I should . . . " In the second fragment a puzzling stipulation is made: "I would ask you to at once remit the money to Mr. Lindon, but as he knows nothing of the transaction, I enclose a note which will explain it to him, if you will send it at the same time . . . "

Dilke no doubt already knew of the little painting's existence, having seen it when living at Wentworth Place. Less easy to grasp is the stipulation she makes concerning her husband. What, for instance, was actually said in that separate note she enclosed, meant to "explain" the transaction, that is, explain *why* the money was being sent? Was that separate note—in Fanny's own hand, evidently—to be sent to Louis? Or was Dilke expected to copy it out as his own? If sent in Fanny's hand, how was Dilke to explain his having it? How does the separate note fit in with Fanny and her husband living under the same roof and seeing each other every day? A long list of such probing questions might be asked, but the answers to all of them really come down to this: regarding the Keats miniature, Louis Lindon was to know nothing. He was not even to know it existed. No one but Mrs. Lindon and the purchaser would ever know the truth.

Dilke bought the miniature, for what price no one knows. It was kept in his family for many years, descending to his son, then to his grandson (Sir Charles, who came near attaining office as England's prime minister). If further Keats things were sold by Fanny at this time to Dilke or others, those sales have gone unrecorded. If she had not died when she did, in December 1865, it is quite likely that her little box of Keats treasures, the love letters included, would sooner or later have been emptied.

Two separate publishing events, sixty years apart, close out Fanny's story: the publication in 1878 of Keats' love letters to her, and the publication in 1937 of her letters to Keats' sister. Of the first, she was both prime cause and prime subject, of the second only the subject. The first condemned her to a long period of posthumous obloquy. The second rescued her from disgrace and anointed her a heroine of English literature. Neither reaction was fully warranted.

The affair of the love letters began as soon as fate had removed Louis from the scene. On October 21, 1872, he died at his home in London, aged sixty-one, and was buried in the same grave as his wife in Brompton Cemetery. His son Herbert, delaying only the necessary decent interval, acting also for his sister Margaret, then began seeking a market for the long-hidden boxful of Keats relics. Like his mother, he didn't have to look far or long, for the Dilke family gladly took and paid well for everything (including the curiously preserved drafts of Fanny's 1829 letter to Brown and her 1848 letter to Mrs. Dilke, both carefully torn so as to retain only the Keats references).

There were now only thirty-nine love letters, Fanny perhaps having destroyed a few of those showing Keats in some of his nastier jealous moods and saying things about her too revealing and uncomplimentary. All thirty-nine passed to the Dilke archives on a special basis. While the evidence is neither direct nor contemporary, the outlines of the transaction can be stated reliably. In buying the love letters from Herbert, Sir Charles was not allowed to purchase full and exclusive ownership. Instead he received only the right to possess the letters physically, and this was done solely to prevent their publication.

Having read the letters, Sir Charles was appalled at the unflattering self-portrait they drew of his grandfather's old friend, appalled as well at the idea of so sensitive a heart as Keats' being so cruelly exposed to the public gaze. Unhesitatingly he vowed that the letters should never reach print, and he was willing to pay almost any price to gain full possession of them. But Herbert would agree only to the peculiar arrangement actually concluded, in which publication was interdicted so long as the letters remained with Sir Charles.

For some two years, quiescent among the voluminous Dilke literary holdings, the letters lay safe from the public's rude stare. Then Herbert in the fall of 1874, convinced that he'd made a bad financial move, demanded the letters back, at the same time offering to repay all or part of the sum involved. Feeling no concern about the letters' content, how they might impact his mother's reputation or that of Keats, Herbert was intent only on turning the letters into ready cash. Sir Charles, taken by surprise, now realized his own mistake: he had failed to get his special agreement with the Lindons in writing. In a letter some years later he comments in some confusion, "I certainly thought I had in a vague way bought [the letters] for the purpose of preventing publication. They had been long in my possession, but the son of Fanny Brawne had claimed them, and I, having no written agreement, had found it necessary to give them up—although what I had bought and paid for, unless it was the right to prevent publication, I do not know." Sir Charles, it is clear, did not comply willingly with Herbert's demand. Ready to fight, he sought legal advice only to be told that lacking a document, he had no case.

With the letters back in his hands, Herbert promptly offered them where he thought his best opportunity lay, to Keats' biographer, R. M. Milnes (by then Lord Houghton). Since Milnes was at the time readying a new edition of the biography, the choice seemed a logical one. "I have in my possession," wrote Herbert crisply, "the letters addressed by Keats to my late Mother (then Miss Brawn) during the time of his illness and up to his departure to Italy. I have been advised that your Lordship may wish to purchase them & as I have no objection to dispose of them I beg, in the event of such being the case, to offer them to your Lordship."

Milnes, in fact, was already quite familiar with the letters, having been allowed to read them when they were held by his friend Sir Charles. Emphatically, even while aware of how much they would enlarge his book's value and interest, he agreed that they must never reach print. The exact arrangement offered Milnes by Herbert, or the amount he was asking, is not known. What is known is that the letters never got to Milnes. Either he for some reason refused the offer, or Herbert grew dissatisfied and withdrew it. Perhaps it was the latter, for what happened next shows that Herbert, or his advisers, believed that the best course would be a dual approach: first, publication of the letters in book form, then disposal of them at public auction. Between these two events, book and auction, enough time would be allowed to pass, time for the controversial letters to make their impact widely felt, to be discussed and argued over, their notoriety and thus their value all the while increasing.

That is what happened. In February 1878 appeared a slim, elegantly designed volume of under two hundred pages. Edited with an introduction by another of the day's prominent literary men, H. B. Forman, it was entitled simply *Letters of John Keats to Fanny Brawne*. The sheer attention given the book, the widespread agitation it sparked on both sides of the Atlantic, in animated talk and angry writing, suited the Lindons quite well. Then with the building excitement at its height, the auction was held. Conducted by Sotheby's in March 1885 at its headquarters in Wellington Street, just off the Strand, the rare event was well publicized in advance, a catalogue being issued which described and partially quoted from the letters. For that stage of Keats' reputation the proceeds were quite good, if perhaps less than the Lindons hoped. In today's money the equivalent of $20,000 was realized (in 1885 pounds, the exact sum reported as taken in for the thirty-seven letters—Dilke had somehow contrived to hold on to two of them—was £543 17s. Fanny was right in telling her children that her old love letters would eventually be worth something).

The outcry that followed publication of the book, made infinitely worse by the "sacrilege" of the auction, was aimed almost wholly at Fanny—but surely she had anticipated this, at last deciding that she didn't care. Not surprisingly, the criticism against her was double-barreled. First, as was said over and over, there was the inexcusable fact that she hadn't destroyed the letters long ago, forestalling any thought of publication. Second, and unavoidably, was what the letters told of her own flawed character in relation to the poet.

Regarding the first charge, the disdainful comment of Sir Charles Dilke in the *Athenaeum* may stand as typical. In a long, condemnatory review he calls the book "the greatest impeachment of a woman's sense of womanly delicacy to be found in the history of literature." Very few of those concerned at the time, few among the reading public, felt that this was in any way an overstatement.

Regarding the exact tenor of the second charge, an article by Louise Imogen Guiney, published in the London journal *East and West* in 1890, gives the flavor. Fanny, writes Guiney, "was vain and shallow, she was almost a child; the gods denied her the 'seeing eye,' and made her unaware." Seventy years after the poet's death, "most of us are soberly thankful that he escaped betimes from his own heart's desire, and his worst impending peril, Mrs. Keats." Scornfully Guiney dismisses the youthful Fanny in love as a "little piece of common clay, the unheroic Ariadne who lost her prince and lived to marry a practical being." How on earth, she asks wonderingly, could Keats have made the costly mistake of loving this unworthy girl: "he must have known always that this was no heart's mate for a poet." Guiney didn't dwell on the flirting and the coquetry, but that is the note that became dominant in the commentary, and "heartless flirt" was a phrase sounded over and over.

Inevitably, Keats himself was in some quarters badly hurt by the release of his love letters. Especially he did not escape some dire censure over his outbursts of jealous rage, seeming to confess a spirit all too weak, full of self-pity, unsteady, and vacillating. That aspect of the reaction was given graphic and nearly permanent expression by none other than Matthew Arnold, otherwise a wholehearted admirer of the poet. "Keats' love letter," wrote Arnold in frank distaste, "is the love letter of a surgeon's apprenctice. It has in its relaxed self-abandonment something underbred and ignoble, as of a youth ill brought up."

In America, the injured cry that arose was even rawer and more outspoken. Nothing comparable to these letters existed in English lit-

erature, wrote the then-prominent R. H. Stoddard, "nothing that is
so unselfish, so loving, so adoring—nothing that is so mad, so pitiful,
so utterly weak and wretched." Meeting Fanny was the worst thing
that ever happened to the poet, declared Stoddard, her influence
becoming "the most unfortunate one to which Keats was ever sub-
jected. She made him ridiculous in the eyes of his friends, and he
hated his friends accordingly . . . Now she (through her representa-
tives) makes him ridiculous in the eyes of the world." Publication of
such intimate personal documents, he urges, should be prohibited by
law, "and punished with the severest penalties."

For drawing out what appeared the downright unattractive side of
Keats' chameleon character, exposing the embarrassing flaws in his
still forming personality, Fanny was not to be forgiven or excused for
many years.

To the great delight of Keatsians in general, and the fascination of
many among the less committed, in 1937 the frustrating blank in the
checkered saga of Fanny Brawne was at last filled in. A long series of
thirty-one letters was published, from the originals in her own hand,
by Oxford University Press. All had been written to Keats' sister (also
named Frances, also called Fanny), just before and for a while after
Keats' death. The volume's editor, Fred Edgcumbe, curator of the
Keats Memorial House in Hampstead, in his introduction succinctly
predicted the idea that would rapidly take hold:

> These letters show Fanny, who was but twenty years of age, as a
> young woman of remarkable perception and imagination, keen in
> the observance of character and events, possessing an unusual
> critical faculty, and intellectually fitted to become the wife of
> Keats. The feeling she expresses towards the memory of Keats . . .
> compels the reader to repudiate the accusation of shallowness
> leveled against her in some quarters. Those who believed in Fanny

Brawne's devotion to Keats have the satisfaction of knowing that their faith has at last been justified.

The rehabilitation of Keats' sweetheart was under way. Soon it was in full swing, riding on the notion or assumption that those thirty-one letters to Fanny Keats were quite sufficient to cancel out all that was said or implied in the poet's own letters to Fanny Brawne.

Of course they weren't. What they did do was briefly illuminate another side of the girl's character, those quieter personal qualities which had helped attract Keats in the first place but which were not always uppermost. Certainly the letters show her to have been, as Edgcumbe said, intelligent, observant, perceptive, though not unusually so, not to the "remarkable" extent perceived by their well-disposed editor. Certainly they show her, briefly and at moments, talking reasonably about some of the books and periodicals she read and the few plays she attended. But none of this is done with more than ordinary understanding, surely not enough to justify bestowing on her a veritable "critical faculty." Those conclusions, naturally enough, were the spontaneous judgments of a sympathetic heart carried away, one that could say with Keats' brother George, "few things could give me more pleasure than to hear that the Lady of my dear friend and brother John's choice should be worthy of him."

What Fanny writes of her devotion to Keats does seem to uncover a true depth of feeling. "My Keats," she calls him when his death appears imminent, and confesses, "If I am to lose him I lose everything." Afterward, mentioning an old magazine that contained some of Keats' poetry, she says, "I never open it for he is connected with every page." But this note of devotion is no new element in the story. For a perceptive reader, Keats' own impassioned letters to Fanny document, by reflection, that same degree of warmth *at the time*, or something close to it. Sadly, however, as she aged she changed, and another passage in these letters often quoted as proof of her finer sensibilities in reality is the ultimate demonstration of the change. "I know I may trust you," she admonishes Keats' sister, "never to mention me either now or at any future time as connected with your brother—as I know he would dislike that sort of gossiping way in which people not concerned mention such things." Contrast those delicately knowing words with the fact that because of her, and her alone, Keats' profoundly intimate love letters, never meant for any eyes but hers, were eventually spread before that same eagerly gossiping world.

No matter. Very soon after publication of the *Letters of Fanny Brawne to Fanny Keats* the refurbishing of Miss Brawne's image grew virtually unstoppable. In a 1949 book of essays on Keats, a leading critic, to then an archfoe of Fanny's, almost gladly announced his capitulation. "I have seized the opportunity," explained John Middleton Murry, "of considering anew the character of Fanny Brawne and the nature of her influence on Keats." After reviewing what he'd written about her twenty-five years before, he says, "I have had the deep satisfaction of being able completely to recant the harsh judgment I then passed upon her."

By 1963, Walter Jackson Bate, most judicious of scholars and utterly sincere, in his standard work on the poet could write matter-of-factly: "Few women have had their memory more harshly treated without justification than Fanny Brawne . . . The hardy Victorian legend was that of a dying poet consumed with unsatisfied love for a heartless flirt. So strong a hold did it take we still find it lingering on as a general impression despite the frequent efforts made to correct it."

In 1993 appeared a book discussing Keats' "Poetics, Letters, and Life." It ends with a chapter on the notorious love-letters, now no longer seen as worthy of remark except when taken as poetry. In the chapter Fanny is approved as a paragon among women, "unsentimental, clear-sighted, frank, inquisitive, animated, kind, and invigorating. Her beauty resonated with the grace that comes of insight and deep abiding affection."

No trace, no least hint of the minx remains.

EPILOGUE: ROME AGAIN

Sixty years of felicity, sixty largely untrammeled years of smiling acceptance, ready assistance, and fond good wishes, *that* was the marvelous bounty that the dying Keats bestowed on his dedicated friend. It sounds exaggerated, but it isn't. The story of the four months that Severn spent at Keats' bedside rapidly took on a fame and an aura of its own, setting the course of his whole subsequent life, personal and artistic. His own good heart and sunny disposition did the rest.

Still more pleasant to contemplate is the not irrelevant fact that Severn himself was very well aware of his debt and felt thoroughly and constantly grateful over it. Even when he came to realize that his paintings were valued not for their own excellence but as coming from the brush of Keats' friend, his gratitude was unwavering. That may in fact have been his life's one severe disappointment, the failure of his early artistic ambitions—very high at the start—forcing him to admit that his was hardly more than a decent, workaday talent.

Always he was ready to express his deep consciousness of his good fortune in having known Keats, which extended even to his children. In a letter written forty years afterward he says he had no doubt that his artistic career "was watched and blessed by that dear Spirit, for I remained 20 years without returning to England, and during that time the Patrons I most valued came to me as the 'friends of Keats'— these have remained faithful to me and to mine, no doubt inspired by the revered name of the poet. The success of my family (3 sons and 3 daughters) has turned on this."

Talking of Keats' last days on another occasion, he described how the poet once turned to him suddenly and fixed him with an intense stare. "Severn!" he blurted, "I bequeath to you all the joy and prosperity I have never had!" and went on to voice his concern over the way his illness was robbing Severn of time to paint. Thinking Keats' mind was wandering, Severn passed off the remark while trying to calm his agitated friend. But in after years, he said, he often recalled what Keats said to him that day, finding in it a note almost mystical:

> It seems to me that his love and gratitude have never ceased to quicken with cool dews the springs of my life. I owe almost everything to him, my best friends as well as my artistic prosperity, my general happiness as well as my best inspirations . . . I do believe that the dear fellow has never ceased to help me. I thank God I am so happy as to live to see his growing fame. It will be to my lasting honour to be bound up with him.

A smiling fate, too, took a hand in the story, devising just the right ending, if an improbable one. In 1860 the post of British Consul in Rome fell vacant. Severn was among those applying and though his age far exceeded the stated limit for such consular appointments he was chosen (his youthful look he never lost, always seeming at least a decade younger than he really was).

His arrival in the city in January 1861 included an early visit to Keats' grave and to the apartment at No. 26. "I am proud as well as grateful," he wrote afterward, feeling the peculiar melancholy of the situation, "to be British Consul at Rome. But I think I would gladly slip back forty years to be again traveling to Italy with my beloved Keats, and even to be in Rome tending him again, for all the suffering and anxiety of that bitter time." The weight of the gathering years and the inevitable silent wish for the return of youth had softened and veiled the awful memory even of *that* long-ago time.

In Rome he encountered a warm welcome from all the authorities, civil and religious, and thereafter, for a round dozen years, he acquited himself in excellent fashion, revealing a natural ability for the task. John Ruskin, a Severn relative by marriage who knew him in Rome, later paid him this unique compliment:

> There is nothing in any circle that I ever saw or heard of like what Joseph Severn then was in Rome. He understood everybody, native and foreign, civil and ecclesiastic, in what was nicest in them, and never saw anything else than the nicest; or saw what other people got angry about as only a humorous part of the nature of things . . . Lightly sagacious, lovingly humorous, daintily sentimental, he was in Council with the Cardinals today, and at a picnic in the Campagna with the brightest English belles tomorrow; and caught the hearts of all in the golden net of his good will and good understanding.

After his retirement as consul in 1872, at the age of eighty, Severn stayed on in Rome (his wife had died in 1861), becoming one of the city's living institutions. Though slowed by rheumatic hands he kept up his painting, some of his final efforts with the brush being portraits of Keats himself, or painstaking illustrations of his works.

"I begin to feel the loneliness of having lived too long," he said wearily as his eighty-third birthday dawned. Four years later, on August 3, 1879, in his house in Rome, the Palazzo Poli, he passed peacefully away. Newspaper obituaries everywhere—once awake to the fact that Keats' old companion had outlived the poet by no fewer than sixty years—announced that "the friend of Keats" had died.

Burial, it was at first expected, would be in the same Protestant Cemetery where Keats lay. But then it was found that the old place was no longer accepting burials, and Severn was laid to rest in another graveyard some distance off. Now once again fate stirred impatiently. In 1881, after people in high places had done talking,

Severn's body was taken up and moved to a plot in the Protestant ground immediately flanking that of Keats.

The epitaph most fitting for the gravestone was long debated, with many admirers offering suggestions, including Rossetti and Tennyson. Chosen was one composed by Keats' first biographer R. M. Milnes, by then Lord Houghton:

To the Memory of
JOSEPH SEVERN
Devoted Friend and Death-bed Companion
of
JOHN KEATS
Whom He Lived to See Numbered
Among the Immortal Poets of England.
An Artist Eminent for His Representations
Of Italian Life and Nature.
British Consul at Rome from 1861 to 1872,
and Officer of the Crown of Italy.
In Recognition of His Services to
Freedom and Humanity.

Identical in form and size, the two gravestones still today stand side by side.

NOTES AND SOURCES

SELECTED BIBLIOGRAPHY

INDEX

The left-hand margins display *page* numbers. For quoted matter the first few words of the quotation are given. Citations appear in shortened form and may be identified by a glance at the bibliography. Added information or comment which may be of interest or value is mingled throughout. Abbreviations used are:

KC   *The Keats Circle: Letters and Papers*, 1816–1878, edited by Hyder E. Rollins, 2 vols., 1948.

MKC   *More Letters and Poems of the Keats Circle*, edited by Hyder E. Rollins, 1955.

JK-FB   *Letters of John Keats to Fanny Brawne*, edited by H. B. Forman, 1878.

FB-FK   *Letters of Fanny Brawne to Fanny Keats*, 1820–1824, edited by Fred Edgcumbe, 1937.

Letters   *The Letters of John Keats*, 1814–1821, edited by Hyder E. Rollins, 2 vols., 1958

Prologue: Second Floor, Front

1   *The Bernini Fountain*: This is still in daily use, no least element of it, or its sunken setting, having been altered since Keats' day.

5   "nervous irritability and"—*Letters* II, 287.

6   *The death chamber today*: It remains a question as to how much of the existing structure dates back to Keats' time. Italian law then called for the general cleansing and overhaul of sick rooms in private dwellings after such a death. See below, 190, for the alterations actually reported by Severn, which apparently were extensive.

Chapter One: Destination Rome

11   *In Naples Harbor*: KC I, 164-65, Sharp 58-63, *Letters* II, 349-50. Severn exaggerates the number of vessels, putting it at "about 2000," all herded into a space "not sufficient for half the number." The true total more likely was three or four hundred. Details of the ship, life aboard during quarantine, and the harbor itself are from Severn's later reminiscences in Sharp. For the sun glinting off the houses see Sharp 59. Severn does not specify such things as the port official arriving alongside, the conversation between the official and Captain Walsh, or the use of a telescope by the authorities to spot incoming vessels, but of course these items are obvious from what he does say, and are necessary in the case.

12   *Miss Cotterell*: KC I, 147-54 *passim*, 165; Sharp 54, 59-60. She later succumbed to her illness (Sharp 148). Motion (538, 539) has Mrs. Pidgeon acting as Miss Cotterell's "companion" or "chaperon," but gives no source. Since she refused to help the young women when overcome there could have been no such link between them.

15   "she would faint and"—KC I, 166. Same for the next three quotations.

16   "All her bad symptoms"—*Letters* II, 350. This letter contains Keats' last direct contact with Fanny Brawne. "Give my love to Fanny," he writes, " . . . show her this. I dare say no more." At the bottom of the sheet after the signature he scrawled, "good bye Fanny! God bless you"

16   *Lieutenant Sullivan and his crew*: Sharp 60-61, quoting from Severn's reminiscences. Among the Neapolitans there was much amusement at the predicament of the British naval crew, bringing a parade of small boats "to laugh and be merry at the expense of the blunderers (Sharp 61)."

17   "all kinds of chaff"—Sharp 61. Same for the next quotation.

17   "There is enough in"—*Letters* II, 350. Same for the next two quotations.

18   "a doubtful state"—KC I, 163.

18   "He was often so"—Sharp 61. Same for the next quotation.

19   "never saw him for ten"—FB-FK 13.

19   *Choice of Severn as Keats' companion*: Evans 338-40, Sharp 45-49. It was to some extent the continual urging of Severn's friend

Haslam that brought about the decision to go, no small under-
taking in the life of a busy and committed young artist.

21 "mental sufferings"—Sharp 61.

22 "I will talk to him"—KC I, 165. Incidents of this first night
ashore and the following morning are derived from this letter.

22 "a heavy grief that"—KC I, 166. Same for the next quotation.

23 *Keats to Brown, Nov. 1st*—*Letters* II, 351-52.

24 *Keats to Brown, Sept. 28th*—Letters II, 344-46

25 *Engagement of Keats and Fanny Brawne*: That the two tried to
keep it a secret is well known, as is the fact that at first they
largely succeeded. After Keats left England, though, the talk
about them became broader and more knowing. See for instance
Haslam to Severn, KC I, 173.

Chapter Two: Fanny

26 *Fanny at her mirror*: My physical description of her is a blending
of four sources: the silhouette of 1829, the miniature portrait
head of 1833, the photograph of about 1850, and Keats' own
description in *Letters* II, 13. My interpretive picture of her *reaction* to what she sees in the mirror is based on what Keats says of
her in his letters' and on all that I venture in the following pages
as to her character and personality, including the documents on
which that opinion is founded. In view of her known intense
interest in clothes and fashion, I take it that I do not have to
prove that she possessed a full-length mirror, or that she used it
often. She was, after all, related through her father to Beau
Brummell!

27 "dress, manner and"—FB-FK 92. Keats himself contributes evidence as to Fanny's concern with "manner and carriage" when
he several times pays compliments on her "graceful" movements. *Letters* II, 13, 19, 40. For Fanny's personal history see the
biography by Richardson, sketches in *Letters* I, 66-69, and KC I,
xlv-liii, also Adami 99-137, *passim*.

29 *First meeting of Keats and Fanny*: Letters II, 8, Bate 423-24,
Richardson, 23-24.

29 "We met frequently"—Letter of Fanny in Medwin, 296. For
more on this letter, see above, 150.

30 *Keats catching tuberculosis:* that Keats became infected while tending his dying brother for many weeks is now generally accepted. See Hale-White 37, 69, 73, and Brock 6.

31 "Mrs. Brawne who took"—*Letters* II, 8.

31 "Shall I give you Miss"—*Letters* II, 13. That Fanny was the taller, probably by an inch or two, was stated by Severn: "She was rather taller than Keats" (KC II, 130, in a letter of 1845 to Milnes). Richardson (22) says she was "small," for which 5-3 seems about right. The only contemporary guess at Keats' height put it at about 5-1.

33 "My greatest torment"—*Letters* II, 256.

33 "There's language in"—*Troilus and Cressida* IV, 5, 54-59.

34 *Move to Wentworth Place of Keats and Fanny:* KC II, 64-65, Richardson, 11-12.

35 *The poems to Fanny:* except for one, the "Ode to Fanny" (see above, 74), it is impossible to date precisely any of the verse Keats wrote to and about Fanny. I judge most of it to have been written early in their friendship. The sonnet "Bright Star" especially fits best at this time: it definitely was not written, as used to be thought, as Keats left England for Rome. Far overpraised now, "Bright Star" is the work of a gifted but *very* young and inexperienced poet, a product of that strange conceit of Romantic sensibility that had lovesick males bursting into tears under strong emotion and keeling over in a faint at the sight of a beautiful woman. The swooning propensity of the lover in "Bright Star" is very much in a class with the quivering young man in Shelley's *Indian Serenade,* who comes apart outside the window of his lady love ("Oh! lift me from the grass!/ I die, I faint, I fail! / Let thy love in kisses rain / On my lips and eyelids pale . . . " Keats is just as bad in *The Eve of St. Agnes,* where Porphyro in the closet "grew faint" as he watched the lovely Madeline at prayer, or in *Lamia,* where Lycius on departure of the mysterious lady promptly "swoon'd, murmuring of love and pale with pain." So it went with a hundred other poets at the time, bringing curiously slight demur. Surely, had Keats lived to look back on his early writing, he'd have had a good laugh at all this himself. The brief fragment beginning, "This living hand," thought by some to be directly linked with Fanny, I see as wholly unrelated, actually part of some planned work—had Keats not died when he did, no one, I think, would have thought to pair these lines with

Fanny. The more abstruse sort of critical investigation tracing Fanny's subtler, less overt effect on Keats' art in some of his other poems—*Lamia*, for instance, or *The Eve of St. Mark*, or some parts of *Hyperion*—does not concern me here. In its own way, such delving can of course be a fascinating pursuit, helping to lay bare the poet's deeper responses and methods. But the results, inclined as they often are to the vaporous and ephemeral, are too little concrete for my present purpose. The truth is, *everything* Keats wrote after meeting Fanny can without too much strain be tied to his feelings for her, at least in part, including such throw-away things as *Otho*, and the *Cap and Bells*.

37 *Keats at Shanklin*: Sharing the cottage early in the stay was his friend James Rice, not mentioned in my text. Rice's stay was short and while there he entered very little if at all into Keats' daily doings (*Letters* II, 127).

38 "wandering as free as"—*Letters* II, 123.

38 "those Rhapsodies which"—*Letters* II, 122.

38 "will you confess this"—*Letters* II, 123. Same for the next two quotations.

40 "Not unpleasant to wait"—*Letters* II, 304. In his letter Keats quotes this line as having come from Fanny herself in conversation, circumstances not identified.

40 "Why may I not speak"—*Letters* II, 127. Same for the next two quotations.

41 "I love you the more"—*Letters* II, 127. This passage, somewhat amusingly, occurs only nine lines down from the one in which he talks of loving Fanny primarily for her Beauty (see the preceding note). The contradiction between the pure love he wants for himself and the diluted form he offers Fanny is only too glaring once pointed out. Nothing else he said or did, I feel, so starkly points up his little knowledge in some things, of course the fault of his youth.

42 "be considered of value"—JK-FB lxiv. The phrase is quoted in the Forman Introduction, on the authority of Fanny's son Herbert.

42 "She wants sentiment"—*Letters* II, 13.

42 "I have no pity"—FB-FK 51.

42 "touched with ardency"—*Letters* II, 129. Same for the next two quotations.

42   "you cannot conceive"—*Letters* II, 132. Same for the next three quotations.

43   "I have two luxuries"—*Letters* II, 133.

43   "You say you must not"—*Letters* II, 136.

43   "artificial excitement"—*Letters* II, 137. Same for the next two quotations.

44   "I am no officer"—*Letters* II, 141.

44   "I have had no idle"—*Letters* II, 140-41.

46   "I have been endeavouring"—*Letters* II, 160. The 51-day gap in the correspondence during August to October 1819—broken only by the one short note of September 13th—I believe was caused by Fanny's destroying several letters in which Keats became a bit *too* forthright and explicit in his complaining about her behavior. I do not think, as some may be inclined to say, that any missing letters were destroyed by Sir Charles Dilke, who certainly did destroy some other letters of an unidentified nature (see Richardson 169).

46   "I came by the Friday"—*Letters* II, 160.

47   "I was in a complete"—*Letters* II, 222.

47   "Upon my soul I"—*Letters* II, 223-24. Some of his more weakly self-indulgent remarks in this letter left later readers feeling uncomfortable. "You have absorbed me," he declares, "I have a sensation at the present moment as though I were dissolving." He ends with an assurance that brushes the edge of self-parody" "I cannot breathe without you."

47   "My three days dream"—*Letters* II, 224.

48   "If you should ever"—*Letters* II, 222.

48   "My sweet Fanny, will"—*Letters* II, 223.

48   "If you ever intend to"—*Letters* II, 224.

Chapter Three: Love Is Not a Plaything!

50   *Keats' hemorrhage:* My portrayal of this incident is derived from facts found in a variety of sources: Brown's memoir (KC II, 73-74), Keats' letter to his sister of February 6th (*Letters* II, 251-52), Hale-White 51-52, and Brock 9-10. That the hemorrhage took place on the moving stage is not mentioned in contemporary sources but is very sensibly suggested in his little book by Sir William Hale-White, consulting physician to Guy's Hospital. It

is a suggestion which I conclude is made sure by the known circumstances. "Tubercle bacilli had got into Keats' lungs," wrote Hale-White, where they "destroyed the walls of an artery . . . Consequently blood had gushed from it; Keats had coughed this up into his mouth while on the coach, and darkness had prevented his seeing it, but the taste of it made him fearful, hence the wild excited state in which he reached home." My description of the seizure aboard the coach flows necessarily from that professional opinion. Keats' act in stupidly taking an outside seat on the stage continued to bother him, and to a friend in mid-February he says, "If you ever catch me on a stage coach in the winter full against the wind bring me down with a brace of bullets" (*Letters* II, 260).

51	"On the night I was"—*Letters* II, 254.

51	"At eleven o'clock he"—KC II, 73. Same for the next two quotations.

52	"no pulmonary affection"—KC I, 104. The diagnosis is reported by Brown in a letter to Taylor of March 10th. He adds that the patient "is so well as to be out of danger . . . I consider him perfectly out of danger" a conclusion which must have come from the doctors, at least was encouraged by them. Keats himself had earlier said the same thing: see above, 53, and below, 174. Very conscious of his error in going without an overcoat that night, he cautions his sister, "always wear warm cloathing not only in frost but in a Thaw" (*Letters* II, 252), and repeats the advice two weeks later, "Mind my advice to be very careful to wear warm cloathing in a Thaw" (*Letters* II, 261).

53	"The Doctor tells me"—*Letters* II, 261. The thought is repeated in another note written about the same time: "The doctors say there is very little the matter with me." (*Letters* II, 264). A good recent discussion of Keats' illness at this time is to be had in the Motion volume, 496-99. Here it is also conceded that Keats' doctors concluded his trouble was *not* consumption. But Motion's idea that Keats himself thought otherwise because he was able "to recognize consumption when he saw it" (497) offers a strange twist on the facts. No doctor at that time—let alone a newly qualified apothecary—knew enough about the disease ever to be sure he was looking at it, even when the condition was advanced. Motion thinks further that Keats remained quiet about his belief that he had consumption, in a "heroic deception" sparing his friends and family the distressing truth. But directly opposing that notion is ranged literally *all* the existing evidence.

53   "The doctor assures me"—*Letters* II, 287.

54   "something wrong about"—*Letters* II, 265.

54   *The heart palpitations: Letters* II, 265, KC I, 103-105

55   "the consciousness that"—*Letters* II, 250.

55   "Health and the Spring"—*Letters* II, 254.

55   "How hurt I should have"—*Letters* II, 255. This note and another written a few days later are the only direct evidence of Keats' decision to release Fanny from her promise, little enough but I think sufficient to establish the fact. In the second note he warns, "I cannot say forget me—but I would mention that there are impossibilities in the world. No more of this." (*Letters* II, 257)

55   "Let me no longer detain"—*Letters* II, 257.

55   "by your remaining at"—*Letters* II, 281.

56   "My Dear Girl I love"—*Letters* II, 275.

56   *The proposed walking tour: Letters* II, 287-88, KC II, 74.

58   "I am afraid to ruminate"—*Letters* II, 288

58   "I have been a walk this"—*Letters* II, 303-304. The date for this letter (No. 271) as suggested in *Letters*, that of July 5th, is certainly in error. That the true date is early June, and that this is the letter referred to in the opening sentence of No. 261 (*Letters* II, 290), written one day later, may now be taken as established. See the lengthy footnote in *Letters* II, 303, which discusses the original suggestion made by J. R. McGillivray in his Keats bibliography (1949). The letter itself bears no date, only the notations "Wednesday Morng," which is probably an error for Tuesday. Only when these two letters, and the one numbered 261, are arranged in their proper sequence do the three yield their full store of information about the love affair.

61   "delirium . . . temporarily"—Lowell 430, 433.

61   "poisonous effect"—Ward 358.

61   "slowly darkened in"—Gittings 391

61   "When he began to"—Bate 646. The 1997 biography by Andrew Motion joins this unanimous assigning of blame to the poet, though lessened by his physical condition: "His illness goaded him to rages which were almost insane" (517).

62   "I wrote a letter for"—*Letters* II, 290-91. This letter was sent to Fanny enclosed with No. 271, the letter referred to in the opening sentence. See above, five notes up.

65   "in thought, word, and"—*Letters* II, 292.

67   *The hemorrhage of June 22: Letters* II, 300, a letter of Keats to his sister. See also the explanatory footnote on the same page which includes the Gisborne quote, also Bate 647-49, and Gittings 400. Keats himself on June 23rd reports the favorable opinion of the physicians: "I have slept well and they tell me there is nothing material to fear" (*Letters* II, 300.

67   "I have no hopes of"—*Letters* II, 305.

68   "shocking and now reminds"—KC I, 121. The observer was Joseph Severn who makes the comment in a letter to Haslam. "I still think he will recover," he adds, and promises he will "visit Keats very much at every opportunity—perhaps twice a week." This was three months before there was any thought of Severn going with Keats to Italy, and he already shows the genuine accommodating spirit that would sustain him through those long, heavy days in Rome.

68   "never spoke and looks"—*Letters* II, 300.

68   "very much pester'd"—*Letters* II, 309.

68   *Flowers and ring sent by Fanny: Letters* II, 301.

68   "My head is puzzled"—*Letters* II, 292. Same for the next two quotations.

69   "many faults"—*Letters* II, 345. The phrase occurs in Keats' letter to Brown, September 28, 1820. See above where the full reference is given. Keats' saying this so openly and calmly certainly points to some lengthy and earnest conversations between the two on the topic of Fanny's shortcomings, and the *many* is especially revealing.

69   "It is quite a settled"—Dilke 11. The quotation occurs in a rambling, disjointed memoir of the elder Dilke. It is not identified as to source, but was most probably in a letter of Mrs. Dilke to her father-in-law.

70   "My recollection of"—KC II, 338.

70   "Absence from the poor"—Reynolds, *Letters* 21, also in KC I, 156. A sensible discussion of Fanny's relations with the Reynolds family, especially the girls, is in the *Life of J. H. Reynolds* (1984) by Leonidas Jones, 198-202.

70   "a connexion which"—Dilke 11. The whole comment runs: "I hear that Keats is going to Rome, which must please all his friends on every account. I sincerely hope it will benefit his health, poor fellow! His mind and spirit must be bettered by it;

and absence may probably weaken, if not break off, a connexion that has been a most unhappy one for him." The writer of the letter was Jane Reynolds, who became the wife of Thomas Hood, and in later years was very friendly with the married Fanny (see various references in *The Letters of Thomas Hood*, 1973).

71   "Miss Fanny Brawne was"—Colvin 331, where it is given as taken from the New York *Herald*, April 12, 1889. However, the item does not appear in the *Herald* on that date (nor on April 2, 11, 14, 21, or April 12, 1888). Unable as yet to verify the source, I have used it here only after some hesitation. The careful Colvin, though getting the date wrong, I conclude would himself have seen the original—the story certainly fits in with the policy of the tabloidish, gossipy *Herald* of the day. Colvin introduces the passage by saying it comes from a cousin of Fanny's, "who had frequented her mother's house as a young boy about 1819–20." Of the leading biographies since Colvin, only Lowell treats of this item, and she dismisses it by saying of the unnamed cousin, "His remarks verge on the malicious . . . we shall not feel constrained to give his recollections unqualified credence." (II, 129). Bate, Ward, and Gittings simply ignore it, as they do much of the negative evidence on Fanny.

71   "an artful bad hearted"—MKC, 20. The remark is in a letter of May 1824 to his sister Fanny, and he adds, "All I saw to object to in her was an appearance of want of affection for her sister and respect for her mother. I sincerely hope she is not connected in the change you contemplate." Fanny Keats, by then good friends with Fanny Brawne, defended her in a return letter to George, and what she said is reflected in George's response: "I am very much gratified to hear that Miss Brawne is an amiable Girl, and that eccentricity has deceived my informants into the belief that she is unworthy" (MKC 24). George's informants, of course, were not deceived all that much, eccentricity being another, milder name for the silly and ignorant behavior—"flying out in all directions"—that had so troubled Keats. George's daughter Emma (Mrs. Philip Speed, sister-in-law of Lincoln's attorney general) as late as 1877 referred publically to her uncle as having been "in love with one who seems not to have reciprocated the feeling he felt for her" (*Harper's New Monthly*, May 1877, 358). Also passed down was the opinion of Charles Brown: in 1879 Brown's son, Carlino or Major Brown as he was called, reacted to

the JK-FB letters by saying that "my impression always was that the love was mostly on Keats' side" (McCormick 223).

71　"All that grieves me"—FB-FK 25

72　"to no one but you"—FB-FK 31-32.

72　"no prospect of any rest"—Letters II, 312. Same for the next two quotations.

73　"Get thee to a nunnery!"—*Hamlet* III, 1, 122ff.

73　"If my health would bear"—*Letters* II, 312.

74　The poem to Fanny: This is the "Ode to Fanny," beginning, "Physician nature! Let my spirit blood!" No clear statement exists that this is the poem referred to in Keats' letter, but none of the other poems to Fanny so well fits the description.

74　*Keats' departure from Hunt's house*: The standard view of this incident is well stated in Bate 652-53, Gittings 405, and Ward 365-66. My own view is that the act was quite deliberate, Keats merely using the opened letter as the excuse he had half-consciously been waiting for. At Wentworth Place, if Mrs. Brawne hadn't invited him to stay, he would certainly have broached the idea himself, knowing well that he wouldn't be refused. See *Letters* II, 315-17, with their footnotes.

75　"was a good deal"—FB-FK 25.

75　"not yet Consumption"—*Letters*, 314.

75　"invent some means to make"—*Letters* II, 311. It is my own suggestion that this imploring sentence is what prompted Fanny to supply her departing lover with the gift of the carnelian stone. Severn himself is witness to the fact of the gift: *Atlantic* 402, and Sharpe, 91.

Chapter Four: Good Spirits and Hopeful Fellows

76　*Dr. Clark and his background:* KC I, lxx-lxxi, Hale-White 77-79, Brock 17-18, *British Medical Journal*, January 7, 1939, p. 20, and the entries in my bibliography under Jarcho, Pershing, and Whitfield. Later Clark became physician to Queen Victoria.

76　"I feel very much"—KC I, 172. Referring to Keats' little volume of poetry published that July—with the odes, among the greatest single volumes ever issued—Clark adds, "I am glad to find the Edinburgh Reviewers have been just towards him." Keats himself records the fact that Clark was to make the arrangements for him at Rome, "and befriend me in every way." *Letters* II, 327.

77 "The great numbers of our"—Clark, *Influence* 69. For the other quotations from this volume, here and in the following paragraphs, see pp. 71-76. One famous building, St. Peter's Basilica, is exempted from Clark's prohibition against visiting damp, cold churches. "From the immense body of air which it contains," he states reassuringly, "it is always of a mild temperature, and always safe for the invalid . . . During rainy weather when my patients were deprived of exercise, I have not unfrequently recommended a visit to this magnificent structure, where they found both occupation for the mind, and a mild temperature to take exercise in." Keats apparently never went there. Well-preserved copies of both Dr. Clark's books are in the Health and Sciences Library, University of Wisconsin, Madison.

78 *Keats' and Severn's arrival at Rome*: Dr. Clark recalled that "I was writing to some friends at Naples about him at the moment he unexpectedly made his appearance here." KC I, 172. Also, Sharp 64-65.

78 *The journey from Naples to Rome*: Sharp 64, which quotes Severn's own record of the trip. The actual route is not detailed but they did go by way of Terracina, where their passports were again visaed (Lowell 497). See also Birkenhead 47-49.

79 "villainously course and"—Sharp 64. Same for the next two quotations.

79 "lively, smart, handsome"—Nitchie 47. For Mrs. Angeletti's background see "Keats' Roman Landlady," London *Times*, February 2, 1953, and Nitchie 47-48. Severn's later dislike of this woman—rather a headstrong reaction, no doubt dictated by the pressures linked to Keats' illness and death—shouldn't be taken too seriously. Another of her renters recalled her as an exceptionally neat housekeeper, personally charming, and with "much taste for the fine arts" (Nitchie 48).

79 *The piano rental*: Keats himself, remembered Severn, asked to have a piano in the apartment so that "I might play to him . . . his constant pain and o'erfretted nerves were much softened by it" (Sharp 67). Dr. Clark, he adds, "procured me many volumes and pieces of music," including Haydn's sonatas, which gave the poet particular "delight." Once after listening to Severn play

Haydn, Keats remarked that the composer was "like a child, for there is no knowing what he will do next." The receipt for the first month's rental, starting on November 29, 1820, now preserved at the Keats–Shelley House in Rome, is signed by the landlady, Sig. Angeletti.

80 *The bad dinner incident*: Related by Severn in Sharp 67. See also Bate 697-80, and Birkenhead 52, where the incident is given in the same lighthearted fashion in which Severn told it originally (but some twenty years later when he remembered only the humorous aspect). Sober study makes it quite clear that Sig. Angeletti did not find Keats' rude display very amusing, her dislike and resentment influencing her later action with the police (see above, 95). Whether the discarded food was really so unpalatable may be questioned (remembering the supposed "villainous" fare on the road up from Naples). The two young and inexperienced travelers may have been reacting—in their aristocratic way!—to new and untried food and strange cooking. Soon after this they tasted their first plate of spaghetti and though to Severn it looked like "large white earthworms," he pronounced it delicious (Evans 343).

81 "seated in his stomach"—KC I, 172. Same for the other quotations in this paragraph. The prescription for horseback riding is also mentioned here, Clark saying that Keats might "buy or hire by the month" from one of the many nearby stables. For a discussion of the medical aspects of riding, see Jarcho 93.

82 "much useful information"—Clark, *Influence* 153. Same for the next quotation in this paragraph. For some discussion see Jarcho 92.

82 "He has a friend with"—KC I, 172.

83 " 'tis the most difficult"—*Letters* II, 359.

83 "There is one thought"—*Letters* II, 360

84 "How well I remember"—Sharp 83.

85 "toward a poor and"—Sharp 65.

85 "had a pipe and a pot"—Evans 342.

86 "cast languishing"—Sharp 82. Severn provides full details of the incident but fails to say just why it should have so badly "jarred" Keats' nerves. The explanation I supply seems to me obvious.

87 "bright falcon eyes"—Severn, *Atlantic* 402.

87 "immense enthusiasm"—Sharpe 89.

87   *Keats and his Sabrina poem:* Severn in a letter to Taylor from Rome (KC I, 267), asks, "Did you know it was Keats intention to make a long poem upon the story of Sabrina—he mentioned this many times to me." Twenty-five years after that, in notes for the Milnes biography, he says that Keats "intended to write a long poem on the story of Sabrina as left by Milton and often spoke of it at Rome but never wrote a line." (KC II, 138).

87   "List, Lady, be not coy"—*Comus* II, 737-47.

88   " . . . as the old swain"—*Comus* II, 852-57.

88   "We are in good spirits"—KC I, 167.

88   "Thank you for the enclosed"—KC I, 174.

89   "O, God! God! God!"—*Letters* II, 351.

Chapter Five: This Posthoumous Life

91   *The relapse of December:* My picture of the dire events of December 9th is derived from analysis of the facts given by Severn in his long and excited letter to Brown of December 14, 17 (KC I, 175-79), in light of his known daily routine. For the events of the following days, December 10–24, I have drawn on that same letter to Brown, as well as Severn's next letter, an even longer one, of December 24th to Taylor (KC I, 179-84). Also Severn, *Atlantic* 403, Hale-White 63-64, and Brock 18-19.

93   "I fear our poor Keats"—KC I, 175.

95   *Sig. Angeletti's informing the police:* Reported by Severn in his letter of December 24th, KC I, 184, 190. His despair over this unwelcome complication of course prompts sympathy. Yet it must be realized that the landlady was only doing what the law ordered, as well as legitimately protecting her establishment. What made her conclude to consumption it would be interesting to know. In any case, it does appear that Keats and Severn moved into No. 26 somewhat under false pretenses, not saying that Keats was a recovering invalid, and *possibly* a consumptive. Of course, Sig. Angeletti must have guessed something of the truth because of Dr. Clark's involvement.

95   "the fatal prospect of"—KC I, 180. Same for the next five quotes.

96   *The coffee-throwing incident*—Sharp 85, quoting a later Severn manuscript. The date of the incident is not given, but I am confident that it was linked to the December relapse.

96   "I think a malignant"—KC I, 181. Same for the next three quo-
      tations.
97   "We complain that within"—Jeremy Taylor, *Holy Dying*, Chap.
      1, 3.3. The second passage quoted is from I, 3.7. If Severn did, as
      he said, read to Keats everyday, often twice a day, by the time of
      Keats' death he must have gone through the entire volume (at
      80,000 words not too long). Other books were also read from,
      Don Quixote, for instance, and "some of Miss Wedgeworth's
      novels" (KC I, 181), along with English newspapers when they
      were to be had.
98   "I prayed by him and"—Sharp 94.
98   "push my little but"—KC I, 181.
98   "This is the third week"—KC I, 182. Same for Keats calling out a
      pun to Severn from his bed. Severn adds that these lighter
      moments were only brief interruptions to all the misery, yet
      "real rays of sunshine they were, all the same, such as would have
      done honour to the brightest health and happiest mind." Fur-
      ther, Severn suspected that these "bursts of wit and cheerful-
      ness" were often called up "on my account. I could perceive in
      many ways that he was always painfully alive to my situation"
      (Sharp 69). Too bad Severn left only this one example of the
      dying man's witty interludes.
99   "4 oclock. This moment"—KC I, 184.
100   "a total derangement of"—KC I, 182.
100   "Poor fellow . . . his stomach"—KC I, 194. Clark adds a comment
      which would later become an item of distressing belief among
      Keats' friends, who grew to feel that he should never have left
      England. "His lodgings are pretty comfortable, and I do not believe
      that he would have a better chance of recovery anywhere unless it
      were among friends who had the power of calming his mind."
100   "He was effected most"—KC I, 183.
100   "Continually in his hand"—Severn, *Atlantic* 402, and Sharp 91.
      Though Severn carefully saved all of Keats' possessions from the
      apartment in Piazza di Spagna, this carnelian has apparently not
      been preserved, more surprising since Severn took such note of
      it. Possibly, or as I believe probably, it was put into the coffin
      along with Fanny's letters.
101   "I light the fire, make"—KC I, 189.
101   *Transfer of Keats to the sitting room*: This is described in Severn to
      Mrs. Brawne, January 11th, KC I, 189-90. Though Severn's

wording is unclear, the move may actually have been made on Christmas day and lasted six or seven hours. Keats himself knew nothing of the troubled background to the shift, that is, the reason for all the stealth, and Severn was diligent about keeping it from him. "No one save Dr. Clark knew of it," he wrote (KC I, 191), a fact that again points up the differing views between England and Italy as to possible contagion. If Dr. Clark believed that Keats' disease might contaminate the sitting room he certainly would not have allowed the move.

102   "and prayed with him"—Severn, *Atlantic* 403.

102   " . . . among all the"— KC I, 188-89.

103   "I have just looked"—KC I, 192.

103   *The January 9th arrival of Severn's letter*: This is stated by Brown in a letter to Severn, January 15th: "Your letter of the 17th December arrived last Tuesday, the 9th" (Sharp 75). He adds it was shown to Fanny the next day.

103   "Mrs. Brawne was greatly"—Sharp 75. Same for the next three quotations. Brown offers this comment on Fanny's outburst: "Poor girl! she does not know how desolate her heart will be when she learns there is no hope, and how wretched she will feel, without being a fool." Brown, of course, in the first place mistook Fanny's remark about not "being a fool." In it she was actually protesting against the image of her prevalent among her friends and acquaintances, that of a clever but glib and brittle flirt, a heedless young woman mostly unconcerned about more serious matters. When the blow actually fell, Brown confessed to some surprise at how calmly Fanny took the news: see above, 130.

104   "turns everything to despair"—KC I, 180.

104   "I most certainly think"—KC I, 188.

104   "cheers us"—Sharp 80, where Mrs. Brawne's reply to Severn is given entire. The complete passage runs: "After the distressing accounts we have heard I scarcely dare have a hope of his recovery, but I will trust to what you say. When you talk of bringing him to England it cheers us, for believe me I should consider it among the happiest moments of my life to see him here in better health." Certainly she meant what she said, yet in her heartfelt remark there may also have been some slight admixture of guilt over the way she had opposed Keats engagement to her daughter.

105 *Fanny's letter to Keats' sister*: First published in FB-FK, 18-21. Preceding this letter in the volume are five others. None, however, is so significant as this for the personal insight it provides. It was by request of Keats himself that contact between the two young women was begun, Keats wanting his long-sheltered, inexperienced sister to have a knowledgable friend. Also, news of his health in Rome was to be filtered to his sister through Fanny Brawne.

107 "two luxuries to brood"—*Letters* II, 133. Same for the next quotation.

108 "I do not want to live"—*Letters* II, 304. Same for the next quotation.

108 "On their last repose"—From the "Ode to Fanny," last line. See above, 177.

108 "I should like to give"—*Letters* II, 312-13. He ends this bitter letter, his last to Fanny, with a wild wish that must have left her shaken on rereading it: "I wish I was either in your arms full of faith or that a Thunder bolt would strike me."

Chapter Six: To Cease at Midnight

109 *Keats' tuberculosis confirmed*: KC I, 196. The suggestion that Dr. Clark's diagnosis was made with the help of a primitive stethoscope is based on two factors: the firmness and precision of the diagnosis itself, which argues a means beyond the usual guesswork of the time in such cases, and Clark's first-hand experience with the instrument in Paris under the direction of Laennec himself (see above, 82). To now, all Keats' biographers have simply assumed that because no stethoscope is mentioned by Clark or Severn, none was used. To me, the conclusion given here seems really unavoidable, though of course I do not insist.

110 *The "proofs" of TB given by Severn*: KC I, 196, 199.

110 *The Italian specialist*: KC I, 184, 225. No name is supplied, nor are any details given of the specialist's involvement.

110 *Prognosis of Dr. Clark*: KC I, 193-94, 198-99.

110 "I can see under your"—KC I, 195. Same for the next three quotations.

111 "Miserable wretch I am"—KC I, 197. Same for the next quotation.

112   "To persuade himself that"—Gittings 427. The old tendency to deny *any* Christian or even spiritual influence on the dying poet is growing stronger, it appears. The Motion biography of 1997, for instance, takes Keats' anguished deathbed complaint about lacking final solace to be somehow a restatement of "his independence" from religious concerns. When it came to thoughts of an afterlife, thinks Motion, the readings by Severn out of Jeremy Taylor simply missed fire, and Keats continued to expect that in dying he would be "utterly annihilated" (560). Even when at his most desperate, in those final hours, insists Motion, Keats "never embraced the 'pious frauds of religion' . . . but retained his belief in 'a humane and intelligent paganism' " (578). Motion's attention to these matters, however, is brief, and fails to include most of the material quoted and discussed in my text.

113   "Severn, I now understand"—Sharp 85.

113   "In all he then uttered"—Severn, *Atlantic* 403. Reading each day from the Taylor book and praying at the bedside, adds Severn, "I could tell by the grasp of his dear hand that his mind was reviving. He was a great lover of Jeremy Taylor, and it did not seem to require much effort in him to embrace the Holy Spirit in these comforting works . . . At last I had the consolation of finding him calm, trusting and more prepared for his end than I was."

113   *Thank God!*: KC I, 224, II, 94, Sharp 94.

114   "I will not give myself"—KC I, 197.

114   *The Severn family miniature*: This small portrait, of so much comfort to Severn in his Roman isolation, has survived and is now in the Keats Museum, Hampstead.

114   "Away from you all I"—Evans 340-41.

116   "To the wasting of his"—KC I, 203.

116   *Keats' calling for, then rejecting books*: KC I, 203, II, 90-91. In this same letter is mentioned Keats' again talking of suicide, and his demanding the laudanum, also the hiring of the first temporary nurse.

116   "Without any more going"—KC I, 205.

116   "I can assure you"—KC I, 205.

117   *Sketch by Severn of the sleeping Keats*: Today the original of this famous drawing is preserved in the apartment at No. 26, hanging on a wall in the very room in which it was made. Comparing the weary but unravaged face in this sketch with the wasted appear-

ance of the gaunt death-mask yields a striking result. Just twenty-six days lay between sketch and mask, so it was in that short time that the poet's features took on their final sunken, hollow-eyed appearance. Dr. Clark himself was surprised by the rapidity of the drastic alteration: "he never met an instance where a patient was so quickly pulled down." (Sharp 90).

117   *The situation at No. 26 in February*: Sharp 84-85, quoting a manuscript of Severn's, and KC II, 90-94, quoting a letter of Severn to Brown.

117   "shook his head"—KC II, 90. Same for the next quotation.

117   "run out for a mouthful"—Evans 341.

118   "The glance of that"—KC II, 92.

118   "he found many causes"—KC II, 92. This same letter records Keats' confiding mood and his unburdening himself to Severn. Same for Keats directing Severn to place Fanny's letter in the coffin.

119   "with my own hand"—KC II, 94. The mention occurs in a letter to Brown, February 27th. The memory of the act, slipping the two letters inside the dead man's jacket over the heart, brought the letter to an abrupt close as Severn was over-come: "I must leave off . . . I cannot get on." Also see Sharp 92, 93.

119   "had a most dreadful"—KC I, 267. Same for the next two quotations. Severn describes the scene in a letter to Taylor of January 1822. It was about this same time that the two fell to talking of Tasso, a Severn favorite, and Keats "said that he anticipated 'he should become a greater poet if he were allowed to live'; but immediately he shook his head and bewailed his cruel fate that he was about to be cut off before he had completed anything great." (Sharp 83). Did he mean greater than Tasso, or greater than he'd already shown himself? I think the latter, yet there is a certain curious attraction to the first possibility.

120   "be made of him in any"—KC I, 184.

120   "Here lies one whose"—KC II, 91.

120   "But is it not dreadful"—KC II, 92.

120   *Philaster*: A copy of this work was retrieved from the apartment after Keats' death. For some discussion of alternate possibilities see KC II, 94, and the *Keats–Shelley Journal*, 1972–1973 and 1981. Bate 694 makes the interesting suggestion that the sound of the splashing Bernini fountain in the square below Keats' window first made him think of the water link.

121   "Severn, Severn! Here's"—KC II, 138. The incident is described
in a later Severn manuscript (1845) supplied to Milnes for his
biography of the poet. The little trick with the two candles this
author tried to repeat but found it to be by no means simple!
Severn says he did it by "fixing a thread from the bottom of one
lighted candle to the Wick of an unlighted one." But actual
thread of any kind, as I found, and should have anticipated,
snaps in two at the first touch of the flame. A half-dozen different kinds of twine or cord I tried did little better (whether slack
or taut). Nor is it at all clear to me how Severn "fixed" the line
between the two candles, whatever may have been the materials
used. Tying it to the wick of the second candle is easily done. But
how is it attached to the bottom of the first, the wick being
encased in wax? He must, I decided, have somehow cut into the
candle near the bottom to reach the wick (though I failed in a
similar effort). At one stage I thought the trick might have been
known to many in that day of candle-light living but then
recalled how Severn had referred to it as an "experiment." In the
end I concluded that he must have had some special materials
(holder, twine, etc.) as well as an inventive turn and a deft hand.*

121   "less and less hope"—KC I, 202, 204, 205.

121   "all I do is persuade"—FB-FK, 23.

122   "She looks more sad"—Sharp 76.

122   "reconciled to his"—KC II, 91.

122   "might have been eased"—KC II, 90.

122   "boisterous"—Sharp 88. Same for the next two quotations.
Apparently it was at her mother's direction that the news was
withheld from Fanny, a decision Brown felt to be very "ill-
judged."

122   "Miss Brawne said not"—Sharp 88.

123   *Severn's preliminary visit to the cemetery*: Described by Severn in
a later manuscript quoted in Sharp 93. Severn says he went there
by Keats' request "at times" during the final days. But only the
one trip is traceable. The poet showed himself "intensely interested" in the report with all its details of the pyramid, the flow-

---

* The trick, it is suggested by my son Matthew who performed no tests, is to use a *tal-
low* candle, which does not melt down on itself as would a wax candle, along with a
waxed thread. Maybe, but I have my doubts. The hardest part is *how* to attach the
thread between the two candles.

ers, the animal flock, and the shepherd. While no date is mentioned, and the nurse's staying behind with the patient is not specified, my conclusions on both seem well justified. The trip, says Severn, took place toward the last days, when Keats had become "very calm and resigned," and when he first mentioned the "writ in water" epitaph (nine days before the end). The cemetery's layout is taken from Severn, from contemporary illustrations (pictured in Gittings 401, Sharp 252, Adami 168, Cacciatore 49, and Raymond 86), and Medwin 414-15, where is described Shelley's own burial in the same cemetery less than two years later.

123   "surmounted by an urn"—Medwin 414.

123   "absolutely starred the"—Medwin 415.

123   "pleasure at my description"—Sharp 93. Same for the next two quotations.

124   *Ewing and Llanos*: Both later visited London, becoming well known to Keats' old friends. Ewing is mentioned in FB-FK 47. Llanos' visit to the dying Keats is stated in Griffin 149. In London it was Gerald Griffin who introduced Llanos to the Brawnes and to Keats' sister, whom he eventually married. Llanos was a Spaniard, and in the 1820s the Spanish Embassy was located in the Piazza di Spagna, so there may have been a connection between that fact and Llanos' visit to No. 26. For Ewing, see various references in Sharp, McCormick, and Birkenhead.

124   "most ghastly"—KC I, 221. Severn explains in his letter of February 22nd to Haslam that "I have these three nights sat up with him from the apprehension of his dying." The death vigil, then, began on the nineteenth.

124   "Did you ever see"—KC I, 224. The passage is in a letter of Severn to Taylor written two weeks after Keats' death. Severn himself provides the quotation marks. The reference to convulsion is not in quotes but is clearly meant to be part of Keats' dying statement.

125   "O how bitterly"—KC I, 224.

125   "My good-natured fire"—Evans 343-44. The unusual phrase "good-natured" used to describe the flames in the sitting room fireplace—low, quiet, and steady-burning—nicely captures Severn's weary, homesick mood at this time. As his letters abundantly show, he had a true ear for the telling word or phrase, carelessly thrown off.

126   "O! how anxious I"—KC I, 220.

126   "Poor Keats keeps me"—KC I, 221. Same for the next quotation.

127   *Departure of the English nurse*: Severn says that the nurse "had been with me all this day" (KC I, 225), but he doesn't say just when she left. I think it is clear she was gone by about four P.M., when the final crisis began. Otherwise she perhaps would have remained, and Severn would have mentioned the fact. The phrase he uses, "had been," seems conclusive on the point.

127   *Details of the last day*: The primary document is a fragmentary letter of Severn to Brown written a day or two after the death but never finished and never sent, given in Sharp 94 from the original (which still exists). After another day or two the distraught Severn managed to finish and send another letter to Brown, worded much the same as the discarded effort (KC II, 94, dated February 27th). A week after that he wrote a longer, more detailed letter to Taylor (KC I, 223-28, includes lengthy footnotes).

127   "extreme" and "not earthly"—KC I, 224.

127   "Don't breathe on me"—KC I, 225. Same for the next quotation.

128   "Don't be frightened"—Sharp 94, KC II, 94.

128   *The hour of Keats' death*: According to Severn it was about four P.M. when the "approach of death" came on (Sharp 94 says "half-past four"; KC II, 94 says "about four"; KC I, 224 says "at 4 oclock afternoon"). For the next six or so hours Keats' distress "increased until eleven at night, when he gradually sank into death, so quiet that I still thought he slept" (Sharp 94; KC II, 94 says the same). To Taylor two weeks afterward Severn wrote, "he clasped my hand very fast as I held him in my arms . . . his eyes looked up at me with extreme sensibility but without pain—at 11 he died in my arms" (KC I, 225). Severn, of course, was not consciously recording the hour for posterity, and his earliest references place it at some time *after* eleven, the moment when Keats' struggles *began* to subside. How long after, there is no way of knowing.

128   "I confess that his"—Sharp, 94.

129   "The lungs were completely"—KC II, 94. The autopsy was performed by Dr. Clark aided by the unnamed Italian physician and one other. What they found they pronounced as "the worst possible Consumption—the lungs were entirely destroyed—the cells were quite gone" (KC I, 225).

129 *Fanny's Letters in the coffin*: KC II, 92, 94; Sharp 93.

129 *The funeral*: Described all too briefly by Severn in his letter to Taylor, KC I, 225-28. See also Sharp 96. In attendance, aside from Severn, Dr. Clark, and the minister, were no more than six others: William Ewing, Richard Westmacott, Dr. Luby, Ambrose Poynter, Henry Park, and an unknown named Henderson (KC I, 227 and note).

129 "He is gone—he died"—Sharp 94. This is the earlier, discarded version of the actual letter sent to Brown on February 27th (KC II, 94). It is unfinished and the handwriting is a scrawl deteriorating toward the end, where it trails off with a reference to the police coming for the contaminated furniture (in a crossed-out sentence not included in the published text).

130 "It is now five days"—Sharp 98. Along with most of those waiting in London, Fanny heard the news of Keats' death on March 17th, and, as Brown says, five days later she had recovered. After another five days she wrote a long letter to Keats' sister which demonstrates that she had indeed regained her usual self-control. Of her dead lover she says "I know my Keats is happy, happier a thousand times than he could have been here . . . you never can know how much he has suffered. So much so that I do believe were it in my power I would not bring him back" (FB-FK 25). Brown is a witness to Fanny's putting on mourning, as did her mother and Keats' sister and others. But later stories that have her, attired dramatically in widow's cap and black dress, wandering in lonely grief at night across Hampstead Heath— "until some watchman, bearing his lantern, at last discovered her"—are far from reliable (see Richardson 87). The sentimental girlhood recollections of Mrs. Perrins, daughter of Dr. Rodd of Hampstead, who attended the Brawnes, given seventy-five years after the fact, unfortunately are equally suspect (see a dozen references in Richardson). Of course, those who prefer to see Fanny as ever-faithful to her doomed poet—even in later life, even as she bore three children to her actual husband of thirty years— are glad to accept all favorable later claims on the point, particularly those available in Richardson. The tendency can be traced most recently in the Andrew Motion volume, which repeats Richardson unquestioningly (see 568-69). He states as received fact, for example, the wholly unsupported idea that through the rest of her life "she never took off the ring he had given her." She

kept the ring, certainly, as a more or less valuable keepsake, but would never have chanced wearing it in sight of her husband, from whom she always concealed the truth of her link to Keats (see above, 137, 148, 153).

Chapter Seven: Glowing Prospects

131   *Severn afterward*: The touching story of Severn's subsequent life is very fully told in the Sharp and Birkenhead biographies (an earlier effort by Birkenhead, *Against Oblivion*, 1943, includes much outright fictionalizing). The two biographies quote copiously from Severn's letters, concerning many others besides Keats, and from his later unpublished manuscripts.

131   *Cleansing of the death chamber*: All the furniture, pictures, curtains, rugs, down to the smallest item were burned in a heap in the open piazza (Sharp 96). Severn adds that the authorities "are now scraping the walls—making new windows—new doors—and even a new floor" (KC I, 223). In another letter he includes the ceiling in the list (Evans 345). The wall scraping perhaps indicates removal of wallpaper, but what is meant by "new" windows, doors, and floors? By law, repayment for her lost goods had to be made to the landlady by the occupant. Dr. Clark managed to get a reduction in the sum, but the transaction put Severn, still not recovered from his ordeal, in a foul mood. When Signora Angeletti soon after the funeral made a demand that Severn pay for all the dishes, glasses, cups, etc., the two had chipped and broken, he seems finally to have snapped. As he remembered the incident years later, he was "at once indignant and amused to find a long table covered with the broken Crockery of what must have been the *debris* of the whole parish. I assumed to be in a mad rage, and with my stick I dashed and smashed everything that was on the table." The landlady, making a hasty exit, decided to take the loss (Sharp 96).

131   "I have tried many"—KC I, 223.

132   "astonished"—KC I, 230.

132   "but you can't imagine"—KC I, 239.

133   *Adonais*: The poem was finished by June 1821, and a copy of the preliminary Pisa printing was sent to Severn with a covering letter by Shelley on November 29th (Sharp 118). Severn's hanging

on his apartment wall some words from the *Adonais* preface is in
Sharp 121. Later, Severn credited the preface with bringing him
additional influential friends, including Gladstone.

134   *The Keats epitaph:* Sharp 109-112, 119-20, 123-32, *passim.* Also
KC I, 252, 273. See also Bate 694.

135   "I shall put some"—Sharp 123. Several times during the spring
and summer after Keats' death Severn went alone to the grave. "I
walked there a few days ago," he wrote Haslam in May, "and
found the daisies had grown all over it . . . Now he lies at rest in
a grave with the flowers he so much desired upon him—and in a
place such as he must have formed to his mind's eye—with no
other sound than a few simple sheep and goats with their tin-
kling bells—this is what I feel grateful for, it is what I prayed
might be" (KC I, 238-39).

Chapter Eight: The Girl He Left Behind

137   *Fanny's revelation to her children:* That this session took place at
all and can be timed to late 1865 just prior to Fanny's death is my
own conclusion from the facts. As this chapter demonstrates,
Fanny's intimate link to Keats was kept hidden from her husband during thirty-two years of marriage. Therefore it must
have been hidden from the children as well, and therefore—once
the decision was made to tell them—it would have been revealed
only at the last possible moment. Since the relationship had not
previously been revealed to husband or children, the box of
relics must also have been a secret. The box's contents are those
items that Fanny is known to have possessed. Her invalidism at
this late stage I think is indisputable, induced by the rare combination of her illnesses, angina and asthma, from which she died
(Richardson 139).

137   "a very imperfect idea"—Rollins, *Bulletin* 373 (the letter's first
publication; it also appears entire in Richardson 166). No manuscript of this letter survives, only a photograph of the original,
which at one time was in possession of Sir Charles Dilke. The
photograph was made about 1890 in London by the Boston collector F. H. Day (for the eccentric Day's activities in the Keats
field, see *Keats and the Bostonians*, by Rollins and Parrish). The
photo of the letter shows it to have been carefully torn so as to

leave intact all references to Keats matters (the upper half of the first leaf was removed, eliminating the top half of pages one and two but not disturbing pages three and four. Apparently there were additional sheets, not preserved). For further treatment of this letter see above, 150–51.

138   "someday be considered"—Forman in the Introduction to JK-FB, lxi. Fanny was always "peculiarly reticent" about these letters, says Forman, echoing her family's statement, "but in her later years as a matron with grown-up children . . . she said more than once that the letters of the poet which form the present volume, and about which she was most uncommunicative, should be carefully guarded 'as they would some day be considered of value.' " While putting the phrase in quotes, Forman fails to give a specific source for it, though it is clear from the context that all his information came from the Lindon children, in particular her son Herbert. Fanny's definitely favoring the eventual publication of these letters is also in the Forman introduction, lviii.

138   "which I can but allude"—Hunt, *Byron* 439.

139   "The time was at hand"—Milnes 106.

139   "Conquered the physical"—Milnes 145.

140   "the thought of leaving"—Milnes 212. The poem to Fanny is in Milnes 189; also see above, 35.

141   "For more than a year"—Severn, *Atlantic* 402. Though published in the United States, the magazine would of course have been available in England. The article later appeared in Sharp's *London Magazine*, xxxiv, 1869, 246-49, but may well have been reprinted earlier.

142   *Death of Louis Lindon*: Richardson 140. That the Lindon children discovered the disparity in their parents' ages only after the father's death, with Fanny the older, I infer from the sparse evidence. On the 1838 birth record of his second child, for instance, Louis made himself older by six years, giving his age as thirty-two rather than the actual twenty-six (Richardson 129). In my view this indicates a consistent effort to veil the truth. I am assuming that unrestricted access to the family papers would have bared the reality to the children.

142   "I have not got over"—FB-FK, 32.

143   "profound disturbance of"—Richardson 120. The death of Mrs. Brawne at age fifty-eight occurred in November 1829, the result

of an accident in which her dress somehow caught fire from a
candle she was carrying outdoors (Richardson 117).

144 "most animated"—Griffin 236. Young Griffin, remembered
occasionally now for his novel, *The Collegians*, arrived in London from Ireland in the fall of 1824. An admirer of Keats' poetry,
by the next summer he'd heard of Fanny Brawne through his literary contacts, particularly Valentin Llanos, then a budding novelist and future husband of Keats' sister. Fanny herself he didn't
meet until July 1826 when he spent an evening at Wentworth
Place. As he wrote his sister, he found Fanny to be "as beautiful,
elegant, and accomplished a girl as any, or more so, than any I
have seen here" (Griffin 152). Interestingly, the description
closely echoes what Keats himself said of Fanny after *his* first
meeting with her some six years before (*Letters* II, 137, and see
above, 31). Keats' adding the words "silly" and "strange" to the
list perhaps points up the differing temperaments between the
Irish and the English poet. Of course, Griffin's remark about
wanting or needing to be "certain" regarding Fanny shows that
something in her manner had troubled him. It is hard to resist
the thought that with Griffin—who was by all accounts good-
looking and personable, even "romantic"—the clever Fanny
quite deliberately set about to dazzle her latest young poet. Their
last recorded meeting was at the dinner party of early 1829, it
seems, shortly before Fanny met her future husband. Griffin
died in 1840, well before there would have been any pressing
reason for him to have left a fuller record of his impressions of
Fanny. An earlier reference to her in his letters, written in June
1825, a year before he met her, shows that talk of the old love
affair hadn't died. "Keats you must know was in love," he writes
his sister, passing on information he'd been told by his friend
Llanos, "and the lady whom he was to have married, had he survived Gifford's (the butcher) review, attended him to the last.
She is a beautiful young creature, but now wasted away to a
skeleton, and will follow him shortly I believe" (Griffin 149). It
made a picture very appealing to the sentimental notions of the
time, a young poet laid in his grave after being savagely attacked
by reviewers, then the sad wasting away of the tender, stricken
girl he'd loved. Apparently Fanny did suffer some sort of illness
in the years after Keats' death (Richardson 110), but the Griffin
mention places it a good five years after.

144   "The question is will"—Richardson 119.

145   *Fanny's letter to Brown:* First published in full from the original draft and with corrections in the Forman edition of Keats' letters (1952), Vol. IV, lxii-lxiv. It is also given, without corrections, in the Richardson biography of Fanny, 120-22 (where the offending sentence about the "odium of being connected" with Keats is quietly transferred to the notes at the book's rear, the reason given to explain the curious shift being that Fanny "crossed out" these words at some point while writing the draft).

148   "To prevent awkward"—Richardson 167. Same for the next two quotations.

149   "a lady who knew"—Medwin 294.

149   "He soon took to"—Shelley, *Tour* 203. Finch sent his letter from Rome to the Gisbornes in Florence, who forwarded it to Shelley in Pisa. In the volume Gisborne's covering letter is dated January 13th, an error for June 13th. Finch goes on: "For many weeks previous to his death he would see no one but Mr. Severn, who had almost risked his own life in wearied attendance upon his friend, who rendered his situation doubly unpleasant by the violence of his passions exhibited even towards him . . . his intervals of remorse, too, were very bitter . . . " The letter is given as a footnote to a letter of Shelley's to Gisborne (No. 48, June 16, 1821), in which Shelley says he has finished *Adonais* and is about to send it to the Pisa printer.

150   "a very false idea"—Medwin 297.

151   "But cunning Mrs. de"—Richardson 167.

152   "wine merchant's clerk"—The phrase appears on Fanny's death certificate under husband's occupation, Richardson 177.

153   "I am induced to"—Richardson 137. The Keats miniature is today preserved at the Keats House, Hampstead. I forbear any too-close analysis of Fanny's note, precisely because it offers so many possible avenues. Most obvious is the fact that the Lindons were in some sort of financial difficulty, and further, that Mr. Lindon, for whatever reason, was not then living at home. Another point strongly emphasized by the note should not be overlooked: as late as the date of this sale of the miniature— probably 1860, but certainly the period 1860–1865—Louis Lindon *still* knew very little about his wife's early romance. In light of that fact, such easy assertions, too often unthinkingly repeated,

that Fanny wore Keats' engagement ring all her life, "until her death," may be dismissed (see the Keats House catalogue, 28).

154   *Publication of Keats' Letters to Fanny*: For the background I have drawn on the Forman introduction, on Richardson 140-44, and on other sources as noted below. The picture I give here of the letters' provenance is the one indicated by the available evidence. Yet I confess to a nagging suspicion that it may actually have been not Fanny's son but her husband who sold the letters to Dilke, soon after Fanny's death. Louis Lindon survived his wife by six years, 1865–1872, and in that time could have found the letters. A sentence used by Dilke in his later statement (see above, 155), can be taken as supporting an earlier sale of the letters to him than I show in my text, and by an unnamed seller: "They had been long in my possession, but the son of Fanny Brawne had claimed them . . . " Those words I think may be read as saying that the claimant, Herbert Lindon, was *not* the original seller. In addition, "long" appears to indicate a period of more than the two or so years that would be involved had Herbert been the one. As is well known, none of Fanny's own letters to Keats have survived, a lack that many Keatsians have always found sorely frustrating. One of them has now actually gone the length of soberly calling for Keats' grave to be opened in order that the letters buried in it may be retrieved!

155   "I certainly thought I"—Tuckwell 543, as quoted in KC II, 353. The phrase "found it necessary" shows that there had been some serious discussion of the legal aspects.

155   "I have in my possession"—KC II, 353. For Milnes' having read the letters previously see KC II, 337. That publication and auction were two parts of a concerted plan is my own conclusion. Unsupported statements about Margaret Lindon at some point having sold the letters to some bookseller, never named, I reject as mythical.

156   *Auction of the Keats Letters*: A copy of the original sale catalogue is in the Harvard library. Its title page offers the "Original Autograph Love Letters of John Keats, addressed to Miss Fanny Brawne In the Years 1819–20." Present in the large crowd at the sale was Oscar Wilde, who purchased two of the letters—then wrote a sonnet condemning the whole business as crass, disgraceful, and an insult to the dead poet (*Keats–Shelley Journal*, 9-11).

157   "The greatest impeachment"—Dilke, *Athenaeum*, 16 February,
       1878, 218.

157   "was vain and shallow"—Guiney 19. For the other quotations in
       this paragraph see the same article, 20-28.

157   "Keats' love letter is"—Arnold, *Essays in Criticism* 103. He adds
       that to him, Keats seems "a sensuous man of a badly bred and
       badly trained sort."

158   "nothing that is so"—Stoddard 381.

158   *Letters of Fanny Brawne to Fanny Keats*: If it had not been for the
       American Keatsian, F. H. Day, these letters would have been pub-
       lished much earlier, probably soon after the death of Fanny Keats
       (Mrs. Llanos) in 1889. In a veiled transaction in 1890 Day
       obtained possession of them from Mrs. Llanos' family in Madrid,
       intending prompt publication. Legal rights to such use, however,
       lay with the Lindon family as heirs of the writer, and Herbert
       Lindon, for no stated reason, continually refused permission. Day
       took the letters back with him to Boston where during more than
       forty years he showed them to very few, at last allowing Amy
       Lowell a few selected passages for her 1925 biography of Keats.
       The whole strange story may be followed step by step in *Keats and
       the Bostonians*, by Rollins and Parrish. See also Richardson 148,
       and the Edgcumbe introduction to the letters.

158   "These letters show Fanny"—JK-FB xviii.

159   "few things could give"—MKC 24. George's dislike of Fanny
       began when he met her shortly before leaving England, and he
       seems to have let his opinion be known. Speaking of him in a let-
       ter to Keats' sister, Fanny writes, "He is no favorite of mine and
       he never liked me" (FB-FK 33).

159   "My Keats"—FB-FK 00.

159   "If I am to lose him"—FB-FK 20.

159   "I never open it for"—FB-FK 55.

159   "I know I may trust"—FB-FK 21. Critics and scholars today,
       more than happy to have such revealing documents about the
       poet, tend to excuse Fanny for what she did in bringing the let-
       ters to print. Some even praise her for showing what appears to
       be literary foresight (rejecting the idea that she did it for the
       money). But that is hardly the point. Looking at it from *her* per-
       sonal situation in relation to the dead Keats, her loyalty should
       have been to the man. She *should* have destroyed the letters, or
       should have made copies leaving out the worst of Keats' ravings,

and then destroyed the originals, whether or not explaining what she had done. In this, those first readers in 1878 who roundly condemned her were right.

160   "I have seized the"—Murry, *Mystery* 7.

160   "Few women have had"—Bate 421.

160   "unsentimental, clear"—Rodriguez 201. The two most recent biographies of Keats (Coote 1995, Motion 1997) continue the trend or, better, complete it. Without question or demur both accept Fanny's revised personal status, presenting her as a model young lady in love, eminently patient, understanding, and devoted. The more troubling evidence—for example, her "odium" letter, see above, 146—is blithely ignored in the certainty that all such negative items about Fanny have been safely discounted. Even her *looks* are now being slowly improved! "Fanny was pretty rather than beautiful," states Motion, applying the term *pretty* where none had before, not even Fanny's best friends. "She had delicately pale skin, blue eyes, and dark brown hair . . . In later years she became exotically continental-looking" (325). Actually, she had just the reverse, dark skin and light hair.

Epilogue: Rome Again

161   "was watched and"—KC II, 324.

162   "Severn! I bequeath"—Sharp 202.

162   "It seems to me that"—KC II, 316. Such expressions of gratitude came easily from Severn over the years. In 1824 he wrote in a letter: "to my acquaintance with poor Keats I owe a great part of my present good fortune. I find it was owing to this that Mr. Erskine first made my acquaintance and then gave me this order for the 'Lear' . . . you would be surprised how often it is mentioned to me and how I am pointed out as the friend of the Poet, Keats. It was the work of Providence for my good, both in mind and fortune. I can never cease to remember it and be thankful to God for turning to good what I began so carelessly. It was a risk indeed" (Evans 348). A year after that in another letter he wrote: "Certainly I have gained more from poor Keats who is dead and gone than from any other source . . . his Friendship and death are so interwoven with my name that it will be ever an honour to me" (Evans 348). As late as 1877 he was still exclaiming on the

point in his letters: "What a fortune it was, my meeting him in my early life for he has been my stepping stone and is *even now*." (Evans 349; italics in original).

162   "I am proud as well"—Sharp 248. On a subsequent visit to No. 26 that April, either in the house or outside, he accidentally met none other than Keats' sister, Fanny Llanos, then visiting Rome from her home in Madrid. The two had known each other when young in England but only slightly. Now they became good friends. (KC II, 324; Adami 154-55; see MKC for their correspondence during 1861–1877).

162   *Severn as British Consul*: A good account of these interesting years is in Sharp 248-85 and Birkenhead 134-208.

163   "There is nothing in"—Letter of Ruskin quoted in Sharp 279. Sharp supplies his own briefer but wonderfully fitting description of Severn: "He was one of those natures into whose heart and mind a ray of sunshine entered at birth and never vanished" (278). Even in the closing years of his life, it seems, there were some who still managed to misjudge Severn's bright-spirited, easygoing way. James Russell Lowell, who was in Italy in 1873–1874, afterwards thought of him as "the dear simple-minded old boy I knew in Rome years ago" (penciled comment in Lowell's copy of the JK-FB letters, Houghton Library, Harvard University). Another caller who went to the apartment near the Trevi Fountain two months before the end remembered years later how "I visited him twice and spent delightful hours in [his] company . . . to me there was something thrilling in the touch of the kindly hand that had ministered to the dying poet . . . he was a cheery old man" (*Century Magazine*, February 1906, 551).

163   "I begin to feel the"—Birkenhead 215.

163   *Severn's death and burial*: Sharp 280-85, Birkenhead 279-80. The London *Times* first noted Severn's passing on August 6th in a telegraphic message of four lines from Rome. During the next two weeks (August 11, 16, 18, 19) occurred an exchange in the *Times* as to whether his funeral had been sufficiently impressive for so respected a figure. As the final, and surely aptest, word on Keats' old companion, let the man himself be heard. "My children are a great happiness to me," he wrote Fanny Keats two years before his death, in talking of his widely scattered family, "and sometimes visit me. I have 25 grandchildren" (MKC 100).

SELECTED BIBLIOGRAPHY

Only those sources with a direct bearing on my text, or which have supplied me with essential background, are included here. Since Joseph Severn is almost the sole source for what happened in Italy, it will not be amiss to state again that in the Sharp biography the treatment of the Italian period is based on three lengthy unpublished manuscripts by Severn. Concerning Fanny Brawne, nearly every book published on Keats has some mention of her, but here are listed only those that I found especially useful or relevant.

Anon., "A Remininscence of Joseph Severn," *Dublin University Review*, XCI (1880), 96-98.

————, "Keats' Roman Landlady," London *Times*, Feb. 2, 1953.

————, "Sir James Clark, 1788–1870," *British Medical Journal*, Jan. 7, 1939.

————, "The Poet Keats," *Harper's New Monthly*, April 1877, 357-61.

Adami, M., *Fanny Keats*, Yale UP, 1938.

Bate, W. J., *John Keats*, Harvard UP, 1963.

Birkenhead, S., *Against Oblivion*, Cassell, 1943.

————, *Illustrious Friends*, Hamish Hamilton, 1965.

Blackstone, B., *The Consecrated Urn*, Longmans, 1959.

Briggs, H., "The Birth and Death of John Keats," *PMLA*, LVI, 592-96.

Brock, Lord, *John Keats and Joseph Severn: The Tragedy of the last illness*, Keats–Shelley Assoc., 1973 (22 pp.).

Cacciatore, V., *A Room in Rome*, Keats–Shelley Assoc., 1970 (56 pp.).

Cavaliero, R., "A Place Too Savage for an Invalid," *Keats–Shelley Review*, Autumn 1991, 1-17.

Cecchi, E., "Keats' Roman Piano," *Keats–Shelley Journal*, V.12, 95-96.

Clark, J. H., *The Influence of Climate in the Prevention and Cure of Chronic Diseases*, etc., Underwood, London, 1829.

————, *Medical Notes on Climate, Diseases*, etc., Underwood, London, 1820.

Colvin, S., *John Keats*, Macmillan, 1917.

Coote, S., *John Keats, A Life*, 1995.

De Almeida, H., *Romantic Medicine and John Keats*, Oxford, 1991.

de Wolfe Howe, M., "A Talk with Joseph Severn About John Keats," *Keats Memorial Volume*, 105-6.

Dilke, C., *Papers of a Critic*, John Murray, 2 vols., 1875.

Edgcumbe, F. (ed.), *Letters of Fanny Brawne to Fanny Keats*, Oxford UP, 1937.

Ellis, O., "Fanny Brawne," *The Sphere*, May 16, 1925.

Evans, B. I., "Keats and Joseph Severn," *London Mercury*, August 1934, 337-49.

Forman, H. B., *Letters of John Keats to Fanny Brawne*, 1878.

Forman, M., "Mrs. Brawne and Her Letter to Severn," *Keats–Shelley Memorial Bulletin*, V.22 (1971) 19-21.

Gittings, R., *John Keats*, Heineman, 1968.

Goellnicht, D., *Poet Physician: Keats and Medical Science*, U of Pittsburgh P, 1984.

Griffin, D., *Life and Letters of Gerald Griffin*, London, 1843.

Guiney, L. I., "Keats and Fanny Brawne," *East and West* (London), May 1890, 19-28.

Hale-White, W., *Keats as Doctor and Patient*, Oxford UP, 1938.

Hewlett, D., *A Life of John Keats*, London, 1949.

Hood, T., *Letters*, U of Toronto P, 1973.

Hunt, L., *Lord Byron and Some of His Contemporaries*, Colburn, 1828.

Jack, I., *Keats and the Mirror of Art*, Oxford UP, 1967.

Jarcho, S., "Amy Lowell and the Death of Keats," *Clio Medica*, XII, No. 1 (1977), 91-95.

———, "Laennec and Keats: Some Notes on the Early History of Percussion and Auscultation," *Medical History* V (1961), 67-72.

Jones, L. (ed.), *The Letters of John Hamilton Reynolds*, U of Nebraska P, 1973.

———, *The Life of John Hamilton Reynolds*, U Press of New England, 1984.

Kenyon, K. M., "When Did Keats and Fanny Brawne Become Engaged?" *Keats–Shelley Memorial Bulletin*, V.22 (1971) 4-7.

Lowell, A., *John Keats*, Houghton Mifflin, 1925.

McCormick, *The Friend of Keats: A Life of Charles Brown*, Victoria UP, 1989.

Marquess, W. H., *lives of the poet: The First Century of Keats Biography*, Pennsylvania UP, 1985.

Medwin, T., *The Life of P. B. Shelley*, 1847; rpt. Oxford UP, 1913.

Motion, A., *Keats*, Farrar, Straus, 1997.

Murry, J. M., *Keats and Shakespeare*, Oxford UP, 1925.

———, *The Mystery of Keats*, Peter Neville, 1949.

Nitchie, E., *The Reverend Colonel Finch*, Columbia UP, 1940.

Okiko, O., "Medical Aspects of Keats," in *Centers of Circumference*, Tokyo, 1995.

Perrins, "Fanny Brawne," *Hampstead and Highgate Express*, July 25, 1894.

———, "Recollections of Fanny Brawn," *Hampstead Annual*, 1898

Pershing, J., "Keats: When Was He Born and When Did He Die?" *PMLA*, LV (Sept. 1940), 802-14.

Raymond, E., *Two Gentlemen of Rome: The Story of Keats and Shelley*, Cassell, 1952.

Richardson, J., *Fanny Brawne*, Vanguard P, 1952.

———, *The Everlasting Spell: A Study of Keats and His Friends*, Jonathan Cape, 1963.

Richardson, B. W., "An Aesculapian Poet: John Keats," in *Discsciples of Aesculapius*, Dutton, 1901.

Ricks, C., *Keats and Embarrassment*, Oxford UP, 1974.

Rodriguez, A., *Book of The Heart: Life of John Keats*, Lindisfarne Press, 1993.

Rogers, N., *Keats, Shelley and Rome*, Keats–Shelley Assoc., 1949.

Rollins, H. E. (ed.), *The Keats Circle: Letters and Papers*, 1816–1878, 2 vols. Harvard UP, 1948.

———, "A Fanny Brawne Letter of 1848," *Harvard Library Bulletin* March 1951, 372-75.

———, *More Letters and Poems of the Keats Circle*, Harvard UP, 1935.

———, and Parrish, S. M., *Keats and the Bostonians*, Harvard UP, 1951.

Russell, S. C., "Self-Destroying Love in Keats," *Keats–Shelley Journal*, V.16, 79-91.

Ryan, R. M., *Keats: The Religious Sense*, Princeton UP, 1976.

Severn, J., "On the Vicisstudes Of Keats' Fame," *Atlantic Monthly*, April 1863, 401-407.

Sharp, W., "Joseph Severn and His Correspondents," *Atlantic Monthly*, Dec. 1891, 736-48.

———, *The Life and Letters of Joseph Severn*, Scribner, 1892.

———, "The Portraits of Keats," *The Century*, Feb. 1906, 535-51.

Shelley, P. B., *Essays, Letters From Abroad*, etc., London, 1840.

Stoddard, R. H., "Keats' Love Letters," *Appleton's Journal*, June 1878, 379-382.

Taylor, J., *Holy Dying*, Clarendon Press, 1989.

Taylor, O., "John Taylor: Author and Publisher," *London Mercury*, June 1925, 258-65.

Walsh, T. A., "Lowing at the Skies with Garlands Dressed: How the Urn Speaks," unpublished paper, Boston College, 1983.

Ward, A., *John Keats: The Making of a Poet*, Viking Press, 1963.

Whitfield, A., "Clark and Combe: Fact and Fantasy," *Journal of the Royal College of Physicians*, Vol. 11, No. 3 (April 1977), 268-72.

Wright, B., "A Footnote to Wilde's Sonnet," *Keats–Shelley Memorial Bulletin*, V.7 (1958) 9-11.